Y

GIRLS JUST

WANT TO

HAVE FUN

ROSALIE WEBB

Dedicated to my dear friends
Jan Rattray and Jan Brooks

DISCLAIMER

This is a work of creative non-fiction. All the events in this memoir are true to the best of my memory. Some names and characteristics of the persons in this book have been changed to protect their identities. Some events have been compressed and some dialogue has been recreated. I, in no way represent any company, corporation or brand, mentioned herein.

This book has been written to give a truthful account of the experience of living in the late 1960s, and to convey a candid first-hand understanding of what it was like to be a resident of the YWCA in Richmond, Victoria, Australia.

I would like to thank the people portrayed in this book for taking me into their confidence. I recognize that their memories of events described in this book may be different than my own.

CONTENTS

.

PROLOGUE

I was in my teens when I first arrived at the YWCA in Richmond. I was separated from my family at a vulnerable time in my life. There was no compassion shown at all by this so called 'home away from home'. If you were lonely, sick or needed help in any manner, it would not be forthcoming in any way, shape or form.

I was changed profoundly by the experience of this accommodation.

The story is interwoven with daily life in the rag trade, the evolution of Richmond, the politics of the Vietnam War, the multiculturalism, the gang land wars and the gender attitudes. This story sits between a memoir and an historical novel.

This book tells the journey. At the heart of the story is the bond that can form between people with different backgrounds and personalities, all with one common goal, and that was to survive.

I describe the struggles and triumphs of young women who came under the auspices of so-called protection and care.

There is a truth in this book that we all need to understand. My life has had so many happy times but that was not the case for all.

During research for this book I unravelled and uncovered many distressing stories. We should all have the opportunity to speak up and not feel so smothered by a controlling system.

The institution operated under a code of silence.

Thankfully the type of accommodation detailed in this book, is no longer available to young country girls. We have learnt so much since the 60s about protecting young women.

INTRODUCTION

Life at Doery House, the Young Women's Christian Association (YWCA) hostel at 353 Church Street Richmond Victoria, should have been a home away from home for the teenage girls that resided there in the late 1960s but alas this was nowhere near the reality.

Research shows that there were periods in its history where the girls were treated with respect and given a home with staff that cared for them and nurtured them as the resident's parents would wish.

In the late 1960s the building had already been in use for some 75 years as accommodation for young country women, with some success judging by the feedback in the following chapters.

This book details many of the stories that occurred during the three-year period between 1966 and 1969. They are all based on fact. The names have been changed and/or pseudonyms used. The stories highlight the trauma many experienced with little compassion from the YWCA. Maybe the hierarchy did not know what was going on in one of their facilities. Stories would have been relayed from the residents to their parents, but the parents would have been well aware that to inform the management of the YWCA could possibly have been to their detriment. After all, where would they have sent their daughters anyway?

It will be obvious that without the companionship of the other girls and the friendships built up over a period of time many of the residents would have found it difficult to go on.

Maybe life at the YWCA Richmond was meant to 'toughen up' the girls but for many the reverse was actually the case.

In the late 1960s the word 'Christian' meant little to some.

1

FRAGILE EXISTENCE

It didn't take long for it to ripple through the hostel that someone had decided that life was all too much for them to bear. It had all begun with Wendy coming across what looked like blood dripping out the side of the bed in her shared room. Jill would have got away with it and her mission to leave them all would have gone undiscovered if she had just kept her slim arms in the bed and pulled the bedspread up a little bit higher.

After all Wendy would probably not have seen the blood on the old worn timber floorboards if it had seeped through the bedclothes. Even the rug would not have given up the ghastly secrets of the last hour as it was many shades of brown and had probably never been cleaned. A few drops of blood here and there would not have been evident to anyone let alone Wendy in her rushed state.

Jill worked strange hours and Wendy was used to doing her best to creep around the room noiselessly before going to work each morning, as Jill was often still comatose when Wendy needed to prepare for her day ahead. This was an annoyance to Wendy when she was sleeping on the outside verandah, but when she was sleeping inside the house she just didn't care at all how long Jill slept as she was outside and not even the clatter and racket of the trams along Church Street would rouse Jill.

Wendy and Jill were as mismatched as most of the room pairings were, and consequently they didn't care too much for each other. They had been thrown together out of necessity and a means to an end by the Y. Like most of the girls they had come from the country or faraway places and knew little or nothing about city life. They were not worldly wise and therefore were not even prepared for the evil elements of life that was lurking in the big smoke. They had both lived sheltered lives, one having lived her life on Flinders Island and the other from Warrnambool. Both these places were as far away from Melbourne life as you could get.

Flinders Island is an Island in Bass Strait between Victoria and Tasmania. It was named Flinders Island after the British Navigator, Matthew Flinders, who charted it in the late 1700s. Jill was heard to say once to one of the girls doing her apprenticeship in hairdressing that she didn't have much need for a hairdresser in the past as where she lived was in the 'Roaring Forties'. The name was given as it was always extremely windy, hence the reason Jill had long hair that was always tied back tightly.

Warrnambool on the other hand was slightly more civilised being more easily accessible on the mainland. It was a great tourist destination being at the Western end of the Great Ocean Road. Wendy always commented on the Fletcher Jones factory being there and how one could buy their clothes cheaper in her hometown than in Melbourne. Fletcher Jones was always considered as something of an iconic clothing store where the astute buyer always went for clothing of quality made from superior fabric.

Despite the pair not caring for each other too much Wendy was absolutely frantic when she realised Jill may not be asleep but could actually be dead.

Wendy saw where the blood was dripping from Jill's arm on to the white sheet, not immediately but only when she had collected all her belongings that were required for her morning trip to the bathroom. As she turned to leave the room she noticed a glint of sunlight had caught itself under the blind where it had not been lowered completely the night before. This filter of light caught the brightness of the red dripping blood, the sight of which had Wendy rooted to the floorboards for a short time. When her brain finally processed the information, she flung open the door and screamed so loudly and so high pitched that most of the girls thought there had been a murder in the Y.

Upon racing back in to the room she saw the razor blade packet on the side of the dressing table next to the bed. Wendy did not want to touch it but could see there were several blades and one in particular was sticking out the side of the packet. Was this what Jill had used to try and end her short, precious life?

It didn't take long for help to arrive and Matron was hot on the heels of the first girls to arrive at the door of the room. She brushed them all aside and told them to get back to their rooms.

She looked at Wendy and said, 'What are you doing here?'

To which Wendy replied, 'This is my room, I share it with Jill.'

Breakfast that morning was abuzz with chatter about the occurrence in room 26. Jill had always wanted to fulfil her dream of being an accountant, but it turned out that the dream could only be fulfilled and become a reality if she was a willing or unwilling party in her employer's trysts. She had imparted a lot of this story to one of her few friends at the Y, being Sylvia who was in room 21, but Sylvia had believed that Keith with the wandering hands and over active appendage would soon get tired of pursuing Jill and move on to someone or something else. This reasoning came from the fact that sometimes Keith showed little interest in Jill and other times he was over attentive in a sexual way.

Was it possible he only showed interest in Jill when he was receiving little or no love and affection at home?

Sylvia's mother had always said this type of thing only happened to girls when they encouraged men, not that Sylvia saw any truth in this.

It all seemed to begin with what might be seen as an innocent over interest in Jill and progressed with simple pats on the back and the occasional arm around the shoulder. Little gifts were even given in anticipation of future expansion of the relationship, as Keith put it.

Keith began asking Jill to stay back after work for a little unplanned overtime. Jill was able to escape these advances for some time on the pretext that she had to return to the Y by a certain time each evening, which was specified as much earlier than the actual closing time of Doery House. But Keith was not that easily dissuaded. He decided, without Jill's knowledge, to ring Matron and seek permission to have Jill work the supposed overtime. This is when he found out the truth about the actual closing times.

Come Monday of the following week he asked Jill, 'Why did you lie to me about the closing times for the residents at the Y?'

If you wish to stay here and eventually become an accountant you will work overtime'. The last part of this conversation was relayed to Jill from Keith's sly mouth and with a devious look.

And so began a period in Jill's life that she had to endure. She could have left her employment but who else would give her a chance at achieving her goal. After all it was the 1960s and it was almost unheard of for females to become accountants. She had entered the job with excellent book-keeping skills having worked with her uncle who had a large business in the suburbs of Melbourne. Her uncle had noticed her ability and had encouraged his full-time permanent bookkeeper to teach Jill as much as possible during Jill's school holidays. Her parents could not afford to send her to University to study accounting but when she saw an advertisement in the paper for a trainee book-keeper who, if they had the necessary aptitude, would be sponsored through University, Jill then jumped at the chance to fulfil her dream. She was not to know that this was never going to be achieved and that others had gone before her with the same shattered visions.

During this time, she lost her self-esteem, her confidence, her will to become a qualified accountant and as it turned out her virginity.

There wasn't even any respite at the weekends as she only flew home to Flinders Island twice a year, and her friend Sylvia was very rarely at Doery House on the weekends.

On her last trip home to Flinders Island Jill told her mother what was happening in her workplace.

To her dismay her mother replied, 'Well how much do you want to be an accountant?'

For months Jill sank deeper and deeper into a dark hole of depression. And so, it was the day Wendy found her in the bed in their shared room.

Wendy reflected later that she should have been observant. Jill was often late, she often looked like she hadn't slept for days as there were dark circles and bags under her eyes. Wendy had even seen bruises on her arms and what appeared to be love bites on her neck. And Jill didn't even have a boyfriend. Many times she didn't eat her evening meal and she was obviously losing weight.

One morning at breakfast Matron chastised the girls for the food they wasted, she informed them this occurred mainly from the girls who ordered a late evening dinner and then did not consume it when they finally arrived home. 'Why order a meal if you are not going to eat it' she bellowed. 'The oven is left on and then someone has to turn it off when the meal has not been taken from the oven'. 'It is extremely difficult for cook to remove the food from the plate and therefore the plate has to be soaked'. On and on she went. This was an obvious reference to the gluggy gravy that would congeal on the plate, or the white sauce on the fish that ended up looking like thick white blancmange, or the worst of all was the stew that would meld in to one unappetising lump that even a loved pooch may pass up.

Wouldn't it have been better for matron to use her time and energy to find out who was ordering the meals that were not consumed and why?

Maybe she would have in reality found out the problems Jill was enduring and actually show some compassion.

After that fateful day Wendy refused to sleep in that bed. All the mattresses at the Y were covered with thick plastic. This plastic crinkled and crumpled all night long, with every turn of one's body it sounded like someone eating a packet of chips in a quiet movie theatre. This thick plastic was also extremely uncomfortable and made sleeping on hot nights in the Melbourne summer on the beds like sleeping in a sauna and a pool of sweat.

Matron informed Wendy that the mattress had been protected by this thick plastic and they were used for the purposes of protecting the mattresses from fluids.

Why didn't she just use the correct words instead of

skirting around the subject? Didn't she mean blood, vomit and urine?

So Wendy decided just to be forthright and suffer the consequences so she announced in a loud voice much to Matron's horror, 'But that plastic is to protect them from blood from our monthly periods not from someone's blood when they try to kill themselves.' 'And while you are arranging a new mattress for me I will have new blankets and a new bedspread,' she proclaimed.

Wendy had no idea whether she got the requested clean items, but she inspected everything carefully before she slept in that bed again. It took some months before she got even an average amount of sleep. One thing that didn't take long to happen was the inevitable new roommate. Wendy wasn't about to tell the new resident what had happened to her previous roommate, but she was pretty sure she would eventually hear from someone at the hostel.

The ambulance came and took Jill to hospital that sad morning. Nobody knew which hospital and nobody in authority would inform the girls of her whereabouts. Despite Wendy's repeated requests Matron refused to reveal any information. The girls were told to mind their own business and get on with their lives.

No-one saw or heard of Jill again.

Did she live or did she die?

Did she have a happy life or was it filled with sadness?

When she came to live in the city she was just trying to fulfil her dream.

2

FALSE FIRST IMPRESSIONS

My mother was aghast, and in a somewhat panicked voice asked, 'But what effect will this situation have on her asthma?'

To which the Matron of the YWCA Hostel, Doery House in Church Street Richmond replied in a very stern voice, 'It will do the condition good.'

My mother and I had just been shown the cheapest available accommodation at the Y which was all my parents obviously felt I could afford. It was by no means inexpensive and it consisted of living conditions which were clearly sub-standard, but where was a country girl to go when she needed accommodation in the city when commencing her working life?

After all, it was the 1960s and no self-respecting girl would live in a flat with persons of unknown reputation, although the reputation of the girls at the Y was questionable at times anyway.

Matron explained that girls from remote, outlying areas needed to be in supervised accommodation with strict rules and regulations.

'What did that mean?'

The cheapest accommodation consisted of an inside/outside scenario. The description and viewing of this living arrangement on a fine and sunny day in spring did not match the reality of a wet, windy winter's Melbourne night.

I also discovered that I was to share my room with an unknown girl – hence the inside / outside arrangement. I would sleep one week in a sparse room inside the main building and on the alternate week I would sleep on a verandah at the front of the building. It consisted of a back wall which formed part of the main building; there was a dividing wall with six beds on either side pushed up against the main wall. The only protection from the weather was to be canvas drop down blinds that offered little shelter from the noise, wind and rain. The beds ran parallel to the back wall with only a thread bare rug on a timber floor some 2 metres from the low timber railing that the canvas blind above was attached to. Those so-called protective blinds were damaged on more than one occasion with the attachments that held them to the timber rails often coming lose.

It was each girl's responsibility to make sure their allocated mat was hung over the verandah to dry if it became damp or wet from inclement weather. Woe betide if the rug fell in to the garden below and the girls did not retrieve them and they were left in the garden overnight. Matron checked every day and the wrath of her anger was something each girl did not wish to experience.

I learnt later that some girls were somewhat envious of me for at least I had been given a bed that was closest to the dividing wall which gave me slightly more shielding from the elements.

One night in April as the regular rattle of the trams down Church Street continued, I realised that the howling wind and rain was not being held back by the flimsy blinds. I feared I would be soaked, not only by the rain but also by the tears that were rolling down my face, and that the bed covers would be blown away across Church Street and into the St. Ignatius church grounds opposite. God surely would give me more protection than those blinds, but was he aware of my predicament in his house across the road? I barely survived the night but soon discovered that this was to be one of many nights where I would be at the peril of Melbourne's unpredictable weather.

I no longer had my mother to protect me from life's hardships. Come morning as I slowly put one foot out of the bed I discovered the bottom of the skimpy blue and brown woven bedspread was damp and the rug at the side of the bed was soaked. I was shaking from the cold and discovered that my dressing gown on the wall hook was also damp.

That day I had the first of many asthma attacks at the YWCA.

The whole soggy story was relayed to my Mother and despite pleas to the Y matron nothing would change unless I upgraded to a more expensive room.

My mother bought me a hot water bottle. She purchased some cream flannel material and embroidered 'Rosalie' in blue thread on the front. Two blue buttons were sewn on the top to secure it. This was obviously intended to solve all problems and to some degree it did. Each night when I filled the hot water bottle and climbed into bed it was like my mother was wrapping her arms around me to comfort me and ward off all the troubles in my life.

Before I could attempt to have the 'luxury' of a hot water bottle where was I going to get enough hot water to make this small luxury worthwhile?

I would use tap water for now but had formulated a plan to improve the situation.

3

THE PAST AND THE PRESENT COLLIDE

I had experienced an extremely sheltered life in the country being timid, introverted, naive and with an oversupply of inhibitions.

I had lived all my life in a small country town that had also been the home for many of my relatives and my ancestors. I had attended primary school at the only school in the village. Everyone knew me and my family, and especially had knowledge of my father's trucking business, which was also situated in the town. The tiny Anglican Church had been built by my great-grandfather, and my grandparents were the first people to be married in the church.

My days at High School, which were to be my first big venture on a regular basis away from the small country town where I lived, were lonely times with few friends, and those that I did have could hardly be called close. None of the friends I made at Doveton High School resided near the country township where I lived so I did not see any of them outside of school hours. It seemed that it was long ago pre-ordained that these were not going to be intimate lasting friendships. These friendships were to come later and would endure for eternity.

As I was an asthmatic I was relegated to the mundane task of scorer on sports afternoon. This was always held on a Friday afternoon and was a painful experience for me as I was ostracised from the rest of the group because of my lack of participation and sporting prowess. In the 1960s asthma was considered a serious health condition without the preventative measures available in the years to come. I did take up golf lessons at school, enjoying the experience, but one could see I did not possess the skills or coordination to become anything other than a 'hacker'.

Considering I was so shy and timid I had no idea what possessed the powers that be at Doveton High School to elect me as a 'train captain'. Everybody seemed pleased, especially all those who caught the train from Dandenong to Beaconsfield. I was to find out later the reason for this happiness. Being train captain meant that every morning and afternoon on the 35-minute trip to and from the bus station I had the misguided privilege of walking up and down the train between all the carriages checking fellow students. It was not pleasurable for me to jump from carriage to carriage in the old red rattlers watching the track whizzing beneath my feet.

It was my duty to instruct students about the need to have their school hats firmly planted on their heads, to remove their feet from the seat in front of them, to desist from running between carriages and to generally stop mucking around. Well of course with my nature I was not exactly a tower of authority, any wonder all my fellow train travelling students had been so happy when I was elected train captain. I was met with 'make me', 'piss off', 'who says' and once a boy even told me to 'fuck off'. I was shocked beyond belief, as I had virtually heard no swearing in my life, but nevertheless I hastily obeyed and retreated to the carriage where I had left my bag.

I was supposed to report any train misdemeanours to my superiors but why would I do that as goodness knows what the ramifications would be. I was already bullied on a daily basis and I didn't want to add to my anxiety, lack of sleep and the possibility of an asthma attack.

All was not lost though while I attended Doveton High. A dedicated English teacher inspired me to explore all matters relating to the written word. I had an inspirational economics teacher who instilled in me a love of stocks and shares, gross domestic product, bears and bulls and anything related to the fiscal year. But most importantly for me I had a sensational and committed home economics teacher who sparked a never dying love of sewing.

I didn't know where this love came from even though my mother was a dab hand with a needle and thread and my great aunt was an enthusiastic devotee of crochet. Neither of my grandmothers could sew anything other than the basics, although they could knit. Not only could I sew but I was artistic, not in a paint and paper way, but what was transferred to the fabric through my sheer imagination.

From the very first lesson of needlework I excelled under the guidance of Mrs. Hughes and it was soon obvious that I was the favourite student and topped the class in all areas, be it by machine or hand. I could make a piece of fabric come alive with my skills in adapting an idea and seeing it come to light. My work was also intricate, and my stitches were completed as near to perfect that I could make them. I had 4 years with Mrs Hughes, and these were the happiest times I spent at that school. If only there were more home economics classes in the week.

The first year we set about making our full apron and hat to wear in cooking classes. I revelled in this task and had mine completed before anyone else in the class. I then proceeded to help others in the classroom that did not have a love of sewing.

Mrs Hughes would often comment 'this looks like the work of Rosalie; did she assist with this?'

Of course, a reply was not needed as Mrs Hughes was secretly happy to have my assistance in the class. These kindnesses shown to my classmates did not assist me in the level of bullying metered out beyond the classroom as the other girls only called me 'teacher's pet' even more, which turned out to be the truth.

As the years in sewing class rolled on and I took more and more gratification and interest in the process of embroidery, appliqué, needles, sewing machines, threads, darts, bobbins, cutting fabric, gussets, mitring, shirring and the other myriad of associated techniques

Mrs Hughes was prompted to recommend that I follow a career in 'the rag trade'. Mrs Hughes had not made this suggestion without the surety that she had a contact with one of the best fashion houses in Melbourne.

I was elated although my excitement at the thought of leaving home and actually joining the workforce was tempered with nervousness and a fear of the unknown. This was nothing new for me as I did not adapt well to change in my life. Enthusiasm eventually won over and Mrs Hughes swiftly gave me a reference to one of the most prestigious boutiques in Collins Street, Melbourne. This referral came in what was my last year at high school, known as Leaving. I could have gone on to Matriculation but that was only considered a prerequisite for students who wanted to attend University.

I felt sorry for my elder sister, Anne, as she was extremely talented with her studies and would have made an excellent doctor. She deserved to go on to complete matriculation and then attend University, but my parents considered 'what was good for one was good for the other'.

Years before Anne completed high school she had been involved in a car accident that had seen her receive some terrible injuries. She took some time to recuperate. I felt some responsibility for this accident even though we were not together at the time it happened. I had been sent to a party to chaperone my older sister but little did my parents know that I was actually the rebel and once I was onto my third or fourth rum and coke at the party I did not actually care what Anne did. Anne decided to hitch a ride with some friends and unfortunately the driver who was the pub owner's son hit a tree in his car on the way down a hill.

Not long after that car accident Anne developed rheumatic fever and hence missed many more weeks of school. My parents made the decision to have Anne repeat the year at school she had part completed. Maybe this was my penalty for not watching over Anne as I then had to endure the pain of having Anne in the same year as me and sometimes in the same class.

My father could not help but compare the results of every school report that was issued during the year. It did not occur to him that it showed what a brilliant student Anne was rather than shedding light on the shortcomings of my learning ability. He would scrutinise the information and I was made to endure more hours in solitary confinement, supposedly to commit myself to a more successful outcome during the coming months. He was not to know that this was virtually a waste of time and that I would only obligate myself to gain knowledge in matters that were dear to my heart or that had a means to an end.

I tried to explain to my parents, even beg that they should let Anne go on with her love of medicine, but this was all to no avail. I did not actually want to be at school anymore and was glad to be rid of all things related to books, study and having to put up with anything associated with Doveton High.

When my parents, especially my mother, read the reference to Nell and Pat Rogers, the owners of La Petite on Collins Street in Melbourne, they were overjoyed.

Once the excitement had died down all I could think about, it haunted me day and night, was where was I going to live, and how would I manage without my mother, after all I was barely fifteen years old and knew nothing about living or even surviving in the city.

I knew that an opportunity like this may not come along again but I was apprehensive as well as exhilarated about my new life.

There was a flurry to find suitable clothing and shoes for my new job. This was tempered by the ever-continuing shadow over my parents' lives with the need to conserve money. My mother kept a tight rein on the budget at all times and because the items that were required for my new job were outside the budget there were many heated discussions between my parents in the evening about the need to be frugal, even though my mother pleaded the case that I had to be suitably dressed, after all I was to be employed in one of Melbourne's finest fashion establishments.

One of the many things I did not understand in my life was how my parents were able to have such a large trucking business but could not afford many luxuries in life. They were not the first people in the town to own a car so much of the travel in the early years was by truck. When my parents were eventually able to afford a car there was virtually no spare cash available to travel to special functions, events or any outing that charged an admittance fee so the car was only used for Sunday drives or picnics. There was no money to go to the museum, the circus or the picture theatre. They did manage to have one trip to the public swimming pool at Pakenham in the summer school holidays. I grew to dislike the Sunday drives as all I seemed to view from my vantage point were trees, trees and more trees. The picnic with my Mother's scrumptious home baked egg and bacon pie was the only highlight.

I was not privy to how and when my mother made the arrangements for my accommodation in the city. This may have been due to the fact that my mother did not want to alarm me. I found out in due course that when country girls had secured paid employment in the city and were leaving home then they often went to live at the YWCA. Therefore, I was about to embark on some of the saddest and happiest times of my life as I began 3 years as a resident of Doery House, the YWCA accommodation in Richmond.

The trip from my hometown in country Gippsland, Victoria seemed to take forever as the roads were one lane, narrow thoroughfares consisting of many traffic lights. They were basic routes to say the least.

But the day had come; I was to have my introduction to my new abode before my living arrangements would become permanent.

4

COUNTRY TO CITY

When I finally arrived in Richmond, with my mother, and pulled up at the front gate of 353 Church Street I thought the outside looked welcoming and that possibly my fears had all been unfounded. How wrong I was.

Once we walked through the front door of the old dilapidated and cold building it felt like my whole world was crashing down brick by brick with every step I took. There was no warmth in this place. Even though it was not a cold day, the place was stark, all brown and white, no colour, no ornaments, no music, no flowers. Wasn't this clinical place called Doery House?

There was nothing about it that resembled a house or a home as I knew it.

Nothing could have prepared me for the cold feeling of the place both in the surroundings and the matron in charge. I had hoped against all hope that in my heart this place that looked after country girls would give me a home away from home. Right from the start it felt more like home detention, allowed out for work purposes only.

My father was an extremely strict man and so I was not averse to discipline and following rules in a home environment. I had been used to only speaking when spoken to when my father was in the home. He was there very rarely as my father spent a good deal of time away from the home due to the demands of the trucking business. I rarely saw him in the morning and not every evening, but when he was there his rules were followed to the nth degree. If anyone dared to cross my father he would roar 'I am going to do my block', this would ensure he was not irritated in any way when he was in the family home.

At the evening dinner table, the code of proper conduct was most evident. Once the family were seated there was no leaving the table until you had cleared your plate of every morsel, no talking was allowed and if you had not arrived at the table with your glass of water then you would go thirsty.

The other reason none of the children could leave the table is due to the fact that the room was so small you could not actually move your dining chair out once you were seated. This room was not only the space where the family ate but it was the room where all the meals were prepared and cooked. Mother worked miracles in that kitchen morning, noon and night.

My father sat at the head of the table; he had the same cutlery as everyone else but to the right of his knife was a thick custom-made leather strap just over a foot in length. It was used on a regular basis to flick at the hands of his children for such misdemeanours as not holding the knife and fork correctly, scraping one's chair on the linoleum floor and talking, which included asking for the salt and pepper to be passed. If the salt and pepper was not nearby then it was your own predicament and it should not be visited on anyone else.

If any of us did not eat every morsel of their meal then they were not allowed to leave the table until their plate was clean. There was many an occasion when someone sat at the table for over an hour gagging on cold food that they didn't even like when it was hot. My mother made delicious desserts every night of the week, so it was worth eating the main meal at the first attempt just to sample her delights.

There was to be no running in the house and no yelling or shouting.

My father could do two things at once when it came to relaxing. He would sit in his big armchair, with the extra wide armrests armed with his broadsheet newspaper reading every word and at the same time have the television blaring. If anyone requested a program he always had the same reply 'I'm watching this show'. His family could not work out how this could be.

The other pastime for my father when he was in the lounge room and he was not satisfied with the programs on offer he would sit on the pouffe, which was situated beside the television for such purposes, and he would channel surf. The said pouffe was not to be shifted at any time and was not to be used as a footstool. It had once been round but was now misshapen from the constant pounding of my father's derriere landing on it. The channel changing dial on the right-hand side of the television was cumbersome and was good for a wrist and arm workout when one was flicking from channel to channel looking for something half decent to watch on the box. My father was adept at this action, but nevertheless would request assistance from any family member who passed through the lounge room, with a plea to change the channel to a station with something more favourable. This would enable him to stay languor in his favourite armchair.

There were a lot of American shows on the television especially comedies with canned laughter. Some of the good ones were 'I Love Lucy' and 'Leave It To Beaver'. A lot of people watched the British comedy 'Coronation Street' but this did not seem to appeal to my father. One show he did enjoy was 'The Mavis Bramston Show' an Australian made program that had local identities and some raunchy Australian humour and skits. My father seemed to enjoy documentaries, and nature programs which were ever so boring for adolescent girls. It was not uncommon for him to watch up to three news bulletins in one evening.

His teenage girls loved to watch the 'Go Show' on Monday night and 'Bandstand' on Saturday night. Much pleading and negotiating went on during the preceding week to broker a deal to watch both or at least one of these television programs. Unfortunately, even if our father gave a glimmer of hope and sometimes even answering in the affirmative he was known to renege at the last minute leaving the sisters in tears. We implored our mother to intercede and act as a mediator, but she knew once our father had made up his mind there was no changing it. We often thought he didn't have a compassionate bone in his body.

The only time he seemed to pay any attention to us was when he thought we had done something wrong or when he wanted someone to complete a task for him.

Once I entered the world of the YWCA I thought maybe home life in the country had been idyllic. My father was no match for the matron at Doery House and her set of rules. You either lived by the rules or you were out.

When I arrived with my mother at the Y we were shown in to a dreary room to the right of the front door. It was fitted out in many shades of brown, with an extremely worn beige carpet on the floors and brown leather chairs that had seen better days. I looked around in total shock and as I sat in one of the brown leather chairs the springs in the seat sent sharp pains through my backside. Had anyone thought to have the chairs resprung?

The room had a musty smell and desperately needed some fresh air. Had those windows ever been opened?

There were lots of extremely old books in the bookshelves.

Did anyone read them?

The battered coffee table was home to more literature.

When had they been purchased?

They made the local doctors magazines look veritably modern and up to date.

I had plenty of time to look at a framed newspaper article that hung on the wall. It was from the Argus newspaper, which I had never heard of, displaying the date Monday 9 December 1940. It looked like it had been proudly hung in this position and had not been moved since. The article pompously informed all readers that the new hostel wing was officially opened on the previous Saturday by Lady Angliss. It was to be named after the chairman of Doery House, Miss Henrietta Gregg. I felt some optimism about my new accommodation when I read that Lady Angliss felt 'it would be impossible for anyone to live there without appreciating its delightfully restful atmosphere'. Things sure had changed in 27 years. On the official guest list were a Mr & Mrs Harry Doery.

Who were they?

Would I ever get to meet them?

They must be important as the YWCA Hostel was named after them. The new wing was adding accommodation for 40 more residents which would take the total to 100. The cost of the renovation and increased accommodation was £8,500 which in the late 1960s I calculated would be $50,000 to $60,000. The article gave accolades to the Mont Albert auxiliary for the new sitting room furniture at Doery House. I gazed back and forth at the photograph in the article and the furniture that was here in the room. I came to the conclusion that some 27 years later the same dilapidated furniture was still evident in the room. The drab and dreary room gave the impression that nothing had really changed since 1940.

There was a register before entering the room which enabled the girls to sign in any visitors.

Would anyone here dislike anyone enough to bring them in to this sitting room?

Long before we sighted the matron of the YWCA we heard her heavy feet on the timber floors and heard the jangle of keys. I was soon to learn that this great bundle of keys never left the belt around the matron's enormous waist. This proved in the future to be a good thing for the girls as one always knew when she was in the vicinity and on the prowl.

Matron was a foreboding woman in her green uniform with the button-down front that only seemed to accentuate her large bust. The wide heavy belt held the large bundle of keys. She wore thick skin coloured stockings with brown lace up shoes. Her hair was pulled back severely in to a bun with a strange little hair net covering it. She was not a young woman and as she had the title 'Matron' or 'Miss' it was assumed she did not have children of her own.

In the sitting room the matron gave my mother a sheet of paper listing all the rules and regulations pertinent to the Y and to anyone who lived within the confines of this fine establishment. Well they were her words anyway.

Matron proudly, almost arrogantly, informed my mother that the Young Women's Christian Association had purchased Doery House and used it for the last 75 years as accommodation for young country women. She said the original building, which had been built before 1855, had comprised of three wooden terraces and later the brick buildings were added. My mother handed the information sheet to me. As my mother and the matron babbled on about the future for me, I subsequently read the sheet.

FACILITIES:

LAUNDRY: The laundry for personal washing is on the north side of the grounds. Hot water is provided over the troughs, also gas copper. Ironing tables are provided on all floors, also in the sewing room. Ironing must be done only in these places. Irons are available at the office.

SEWING MACHINES are in sewing room on ground floor. Bobbins and needles may be purchased at the office. Girls with own machines are asked to leave them in the office with name clearly shown.

TELEVISION is in the TV room on ground floor.

LOCKERS are available at 30c. per year, they are situated in the Study and the Ironing Bay on the first floor. They are handy for keeping of money and valuables.

HAIR DRYERS: The use of a hair dryer is available. There is a basin in the laundry for hair washing.

GUESTS: Residents who wish to invite a guest for a meal may do so by advising matron on duty not later than mid-day, if possible. Charge is 55c.
Residents may also entertain guests (male or female) in the Common Room on ground floor, by requesting permission of the Supervisor on duty. All guests are

required to leave by 10 p.m. Supper may also be obtained for cost of 5c.

TELEPHONES:
42-1937 for the use of residents
42-1939 for the use of office
Residents are requested to answer a ringing telephone, and to limit conversations to five minutes. TRUNK LINE CALLS must be booked through the office and paid for.
Extensions, if any, must be reported. Telephone calls inward and outward are not permitted after 10 p.m.

Y.W.C.A. MEMBERSHIP

Membership of the Y.W.C.A. is required for residents of residences.
The programme of the Melbourne Y.W.C.A. covers a wide range of activities. Contact the Supervisor or Housing Secretary for further details.

CLOSING TIMES

Monday	*..*	*..*	*..10 p.m.*
Tuesday and Thursdays	*..*		*..11.30 p.m.*
Wednesday and Friday	*..*		*12 midnight.*
Saturday	*..*	*..*	*..12.30 a.m.*
Sunday	*..*	*..*	*..11 p.m*

PLEASE

1. Be properly dressed for meals. SHORTS ARE NOT acceptable in the dining room. Hair in pins or rollers must be covered with scarf.
2. Place all cigarette butts and ash in an ash tray.
3. DO NOT DROP ON FLOOR.
4. Do not SMOKE IN DINING ROOM or whilst in bed.
5. Sign Day book when you leave the Residence, even for a few minutes.
   Sign week-end book if you are away for the weekend.
6. Use bathroom nearest to your room, and limit use to approximately 10 minutes.
7. Pay Board regularly, one week in advance. Board is received from 6.30 p.m – 8.30 p.m. each Monday, Wednesday, Thursday and Friday.
8. Be quiet after 11 pm each evening.

PLEASE DO NOT

1. Use any private electric equipment in your room, without permission of Supervisor. Radios are permitted, provided volume is kept low and switched off at 11.00 p.m.
2. A radio licence is required by P.M.G.
3. Under any circumstances bring alcoholic liquor of any description on the premises. THIS IS STRICTLY FORBIDDEN.
4. Use basins in bathrooms for tinting or colouring hair. A stainless-steel basin is provided in laundry.
5. Remove any crockery or cutlery from the dining room.
6. Stand at gate or in front of residence, talking to friends.

It is fortunate they put these details in printed form as I was in such a state of shock I could remember very little of the discussions that took place. Some things came to mind as I tried to take in the details of the rules and regulations. One thing that did creep in to my thoughts was the substandard information sheet completed by the person in the office.

Didn't anyone proofread it, check the spelling, check the set out or check the English expression before it was deemed suitable for the residents?

Neither my Commercial Principles teacher nor my English teacher at High School would have been impressed if one of their charges had produced such material. I was also to discover that the list was only the tip of the iceberg as there were many more rules to adhere to than those listed on the sheet.

My mother and I were shown an enormous dining room where all the meals were taken. It had timber floors, was colourless and cold. There was nothing homely or inviting about it and it did not resemble anything I was familiar with. Even though my father had been a strict disciplinarian I had always found the kitchen of our home to be warm and filled with the most wonderful smells, and of course my loving mother was ever present.

They were taken down a long hallway and on the right they were shown the television room which housed more uncomfortable looking chairs and a very old television set. It was like a box on legs. The cabinet looked like veneered fake timber. It tipped back slightly on an angle and then had four spindly legs that hardly looked like they would carry the weight of the old dilapidated clunker. It had a dodgy picture and my father later said that the picture tube was "probably on its last legs".

How would the Y afford a new picture tube?

The dials were along the side of the television, but they had been so overworked that often they didn't operate unless you held your tongue the right way. Obviously a bit of brute strength was also required as I discovered later that another resident Lesley, who was well built and muscular, did not seem to have any trouble with this offending piece of furniture, even when the knobs fell off.

The room looked slightly more inviting than the guest's sitting room near the front door although it was still very dark. It had timber floors that groaned after years of pounding feet trampling on the boards. There was one very thin, thread bare, worn rug in the middle of the room. It did not look like it had ever been cleaned and was in desperate need of replacement. The blinds at the windows had also seen better days, some stayed permanently down, some stayed permanently up and those that did still have some working parts were only slightly effective at best. The seating was a mishmash of old broken-down armchairs and upright chairs, none of which matched. They looked like they had been picked up at the local opportunity shop or been donated.

I did ascertain as time went on that the YWCA must

have been one of the first buildings in the area as the new township of Richmond was surveyed by Robert Hoddle in 1837. This new town was also called the Hill or Richmond Hill and in 1839 25 acre lots were auctioned. Speculators and Investors from Melbourne and Sydney paid high prices for lots on the Hill. The Hill was said to be an ideal place for a gentleman's residence especially as it had prominent views and was close to the Yarra but was free from flooding. This became obvious when one walked past all the stately homes in the area.

After what seemed like an eternity it was finally time to go home and spend the next couple of weeks preparing for my future life in Richmond. At that time, I did not realise it would stretch out for 3 long years. It was probably best I did not know anyway.

5

THE ROOMS WITHIN

When I arrived on that sunny day to begin my life at Doery House I was shown up a flight of stairs to my room. It was not the one I had seen when I first came with my mother two weeks earlier to inspect my new abode but there wasn't much difference except that it was on the other side of the hallway and was much darker than the one I had originally been shown. It still only had one single iron bed, two old timber wardrobes, two battered dressing tables, one frayed mat, one light bulb hanging from the ceiling and a bedspread in shades of brown and dirty blue. Nothing more, nothing less. There were no power points in the rooms and only one single low wattage globe hanging from a cable in the middle of the room. One obviously had to pull the cord near the cable hanging from the ceiling to turn the light on and off.

The rules informed girls they were not to have private electric equipment in their rooms, but this rule was pointless as there weren't any power points in the rooms. The girls were allowed to have a portable radio or a transistor radio in their room, both of which were powered by batteries. They were informed when entering residence at the YWCA that they must obtain a radio licence from the PMG. It came to light that the license cost $14.00, this was more than a week's wage. I decided quickly to take my chances on this and even though I considered myself to be an honest girl I did not see how it would ever be discovered that I did not have a licence for my little portable transistor radio.

It looked like my roommate had already settled in or had been in residence for some time as there was a variety of paraphernalia on one of the dressing tables. There were also items hanging out of every drawer in what must be her dressing table. The old worn mirror that had the silver showing through had splattering's of makeup, hair spray and face cream on it. Shoes were in various spots on the floor and it was obvious that it was not a priority to keep them in a tidy manner. I had not met my roommate, but I had already formed a picture of a lazy slob that was not going to be easy to live with.

A couple of hours later I met Ronnie who seemed like a pleasant enough person, but my intuition had been right, and I was to find out my roommates many failings in the coming weeks.

The first thing I did discover is that my first week at Doery House should have been inside the hostel and not on the verandah. Ronnie was quick to inform me when we first set eyes on each other that my first week was to be outside and not inside as Ronnie had slept on the verandah the previous week. I was not diligent or judicious enough to realise only a fool would sleep on that draughty, scary verandah with the dodgy floorboards when the inside bed was vacant. Inside did not afford many luxuries although it did have 4 walls that were secured to the floor and not open to the outside elements.

On the second week when I finally made it inside it became evident that even though my Nana's house didn't have many luxuries it was one hundred percent better than this which was big on drabness and short on niceties.

I rapidly found that my roommate did not have any scruples and believed that stealing was okay. In her mind what was my property was for Ronnie's use also. Ronnie was obviously short of money as were the majority of residents but the lengths she would go to relieve me of anything that was my property knew no bounds. I rapidly became aware that the key in the wardrobe was there for a purpose and was the only defence against people like Ronnie.

In the early days I tolerated Ronnie's indiscretions but after many heated discussions I decided to fight fire with fire.

Ronnie stole the basics, tissues, shampoo and soap. She used my hairbrush and comb which left clumps of her long dark brown hair hanging in it. She borrowed clothes and put them back in the wardrobe creased and soiled. Things came to a head when she stole my new stockings and put them back in the cupboard with several ladder runs evident. I decided to use the lock on my wardrobe every time I left the room, even if I was going to the bathroom. I started leaving my laddered stockings in the keyless dressing table for Ronnie to

46

steal. I also decided to make a number of Ronnie's personal items vanish only to have them reappear several weeks later in some obscure place in the room. When Ronnie's slothfulness finally bubbled to the surface in the form of taking my clean linen and replacing it with her own dirty linen because she had been too lazy to take her linen for exchange on Friday morning then I decided revenge was the best option.

I spent a lot of my spare time in the evening in the sewing room opposite the phone bay. When Ronnie received a phone call I was always asked if Ronnie was home. 'No', I would reply 'but I will pass on the message'. When the handwritten message came to me I would rip it up and put it in the bin. If ever I was quizzed by Ronnie, I feigned forgetfulness or being without knowledge on the matter. Ronnie soon learnt not to mess with me as there were consequences. It was obvious she did not believe my excuses as it came to a head when I didn't pass on a message from Ronnie's employer. When confronted with this I told Ronnie 'my memory might return if you stop messing with my belongings in the room' and from this time a truce of sorts was formed between us. I never trusted her and continued to lock my wardrobe, but things did improve somewhat between us.

I longed for the day when I could get away from the inside, outside arrangement and be rid of Ronnie forever.

I heard lots of stories from other girls who had roommates that were not to their liking. Requests to move usually fell on deaf ears and very few girls could afford a single room. Some roommates were downright nasty pieces of work and had the bad language to match. Thankfully Ronnie kept her swearing to a minimum.

When I entered, for my first meal, the great cold room with the timber floors and the long tables with the uncomfortably hard chairs, I decided the best policy was to follow the lead of everyone else. I sat alone and as no one spoke to me then I did not speak to anyone either. Slowly the situation improved though, because after all one had to have someone to complain to about the food and to share the day's events with.

My first meal at the Y consisted of corned beef that was edible, but the vegetables consisted of the most awful cabbage, carrots and yellow coloured peas that had all had the life boiled out of them. The cabbage was smelly and colourless by the time it arrived at the table. The potato was lumpy and unlike the other vegetables it had been undercooked and therefore was a grainy texture. The parsley sauce was cold and gluggy and looked like it had been dropped from a high height on to the side of the corned beef. The one saving grace for the meal was the baked apple for dessert. It was well cooked with some lovely sultanas down the middle where the core had been taken out. The custard certainly wasn't like any that my mother had dished up but at least if you could manage to get your tongue through the lumps the flavour wasn't too bad, probably because the cook had not spared the sugar when preparing the pudding for the night.

While lying in bed that night I had thought that maybe the cook who lumbered along in the kitchen with her cooking implements was having a bad night and this was not her usual calibre but this turned out not to be the case. The standard set on the first night did not vary much at all.

Sitting on one of the shelves in the kitchen was 'Mrs Beetson's Book of Household Management'. I remembered my grandmother having one of these books and it was a hive of information which was regularly referred to. It had lots and lots of household tips and very importantly had hundreds of recipes with illustrations included. In the three years I was at the hostel that book did not appear to shift from its original position once, therefore one came to the conclusion that it was just for show or that cook felt she knew everything there was to know about running a household of this size, and therefore did not need to glean any information from the covers and missives of Mrs Isabella Beetson.

I was to learn over the coming weeks that all the vegetables would be overcooked and tasteless no matter what was served. The peas were so overdone that their original green colour had turned to yellow. Sometimes the cook would serve Deb instant mashed potato which was an improvement on the real thing because even she couldn't make that lumpy. Sometimes they served curried sausages and gravy at the Y. Other times they had savoury mince on toast as a change from meat and vegetables. They even had stew some nights which was bearable if the fat and gristle had been removed.

Thankfully every night there was two courses and so one got the chance to rid themselves of the unpleasant taste of the main course when the dessert was served. Bread and butter pudding was a familiar dessert along with steamed puddings of various descriptions.

On Friday evenings the girls were served steamed fish. Fish was always served on Friday nights and the girls received it whether they were of the catholic faith or not. Very few girls were still in residence at the Y on Friday nights, having gone home for the weekend, so consequently only a small number got to eat fish while in residence. There was one treat for the girls who were unfortunate enough to have to spend the weekend at the Y, they were served a Sunday roast for the midday meal. The meat was always different, and I was informed that the cook excelled with this meal, probably because she had plenty of time and only had to cook for a few girls and the scaled back weekend staff. The dessert for Sunday lunch never varied, being tinned fruit salad with a dollop of cream as a treat.

In the winter the cook or kitchen hand served soup from a large, battered pot and an equally battered ladle. There was pea and ham, and consommés and vegetable soup with barley in it.

As always the barley in the soup would make me gag. This went way back to my early childhood when I stayed at my Nana's. I was frequently served barley soup when my sisters and I visited because it was cheap. If we stayed for any length of time over the school holidays then I was given barley soup every day. For some unknown reason it made me want to vomit and on some occasions this actually occurred for which I was castigated by Nana. Hiding the barley in a handkerchief or hiding it in a pot plant helped but did not get rid of the volume served. My Nana sadly did not help in the continual dislike of barley but continued to serve it. Nana always told my mother that I needed more discipline and that my table manners were disagreeable.

The only beverage at the evening meal at the YWCA was water. This was self-serve from the side table with the greatest array of odd glasses for use. Whatever happened to the rest of the sets? For breakfast the residents could have weak tea that had been over brewed in a large, very battered teapot, and for supper the girls had cheap watery hot chocolate. Sometimes it was best not to drink this potion as it could mean a trip in the middle of the night to the cold concrete toilets.

Along with the hot chocolate for supper there was a selection of dry biscuits, fruit cake or plain Madera cake with icing and coconut sprinkled on top. Surprisingly nobody had managed to mess up the cooking of these items, so most girls partook of supper in the old television room.

The best meal of the day appeared to be breakfast where there were corn flakes, scrambled eggs and sometimes even toad in the hole. The scrambled eggs were made from powdered eggs but somehow were edible enough. The girls were served very nice porridge in winter with sugar and milk. Each girl was allowed a maximum of 2 slices of almost cold toast, made from white bread that was placed on the toast racks. There was vegemite, marmalade or honey to spread on the toast.

One blessing I found was that they did not have set nights for set meals so one never knew what would be served on a particular night. The anticipation of something different or delicious kept all the girls interested even if most nights they were bitterly disappointed. They spent these times talking about the meals their mother served and how much they missed some decent home cooking.

I discovered that many of the girls bought treats from the local milk bar to enhance their meagre and boring diet, many of them enjoying twisties, wagon wheels, polly waffles, hot Four'N Twenty pies, Peter's ice-cream, snowballs, macaroons, sponge fingers, tutti-frutti, assorted sweets, and even chocolate biscuits. Unfortunately, my finances could not stretch to such pleasures, so I relied on others to share their snacks with me.

I was thankful that my mother usually gave me some delicacies each Sunday night to take back to the Y. These treats also helped with the never dying homesickness that I felt.

Slowly I fell in to a routine peppered by events I had never imagined in my short life. I had been used to a mother who provided all the things in life that a 15-year-old could want. Even though the family had been on a strict budget I never felt as if I was missing out on anything.

I hadn't even done my own washing at home let alone the ironing. My mother was a wonderful cook who provided hearty and delicious meals in large quantities. I soon became aware that this had all come to an end, well at least during weekdays.

6

NEW BEGINNINGS

If living at the YWCA and trying to settle in to a completely new way of life wasn't bad enough I had to encounter Melbourne's busy streets, public transport that I had never used before and my first real job all in the one day.

I had only been at Doery House two days and it was time to tackle tasks that were all foreign to me. I didn't even know how to buy a train ticket let alone find my way to 165 Collins Street.

I managed to get myself out of bed on time thanks to the little travel alarm clock that my mother had given me. It was in a small brown leather case and the clock part would fold inside the case to protect the face when not being used. I thought it had belonged to my father at some stage.

I had been dozing on and off lying on the rickety iron bed on the verandah. There had been a constant rattle of the trams in Church Street since the early hours of the morning.

I found my way to the antiquated bathroom that had a shower cubicle divided in to two sections. They were made of solid concrete without the luxury of tiled walls.

There was a single rusty shower head that spluttered and spurted what passed for barely warm water. Maybe this was a ploy to reduce the amount of water used and the time the girls spent in the shower. I had to stand on an elevated wooden stand that was not unlike a trivet for humans.

What was the purpose of this apparatus?

Didn't soggy timber also harbour the tinea virus?

The other section of the cubicle was where I placed my clothes. I was not to know at this stage that these conditions were bearable in the summer but the cold, chilly Melbourne winters would create a whole new slant on the term that many of the girls used 'like showering at the North Pole'.

I had already learnt that Doery House had been built prior to 1855 and was considered 'Victorian'. It was considered a 'pair of houses'. It was deemed by some that the internal joinery was of exceptional quality, although at the time I would have preferred heating rather than fine timberwork.

I dressed in what I thought would be appropriate for employment at a Collins Street fashion house but as there were no mirrors I wasn't to know that I was lucky the La Petite workroom was out of sight of the customers. I had very few clothes but prided myself on being neat, clean and tidy, and above all I always wore stockings. These were not an inexpensive item so I was careful to make them survive as long as possible, even taking to darning any holes in the feet section that could not be seen. This was another reason I did not want my roommate borrowing my precious leg wear.

I arrived at the Y with only two pairs of shoes, one black flat pair and one pair of red high heels. I had begged my mother for the red shoes as I was tired of wearing the same old dowdy shoes. I realised that my begging had bordered on nagging and recognised that my mother had only relented to keep me quiet. I had imagined that these much sought after shoes would be fashionable for my working life but it became apparent quite quickly that I was to spend a considerable amount of time on my feet and that they would cop a belting.

I was constantly up and down the stairs from the finishing room where I spent the majority of the day, to the tailoring section downstairs, or to the milliner, or the countless trips to suppliers for fabrics and accessories that La Petite did not have in stock. I ran all over Melbourne for items, to Clegs in Elizabeth Street, to the Job Warehouse in Bourke Street and even to George's, which was almost opposite the boutique, to procure some unusual item. Clegs was my favoured store and it was always the first store to call on as it seemed to sell absolutely everything. They had all matter of haberdashery and the fabric choices were endless, especially the range of bridal fabrics which were a wonder to behold.

Thankfully when Melbourne had been surveyed in the 1800s they had laid out the streets in grids. I blessed these designers of the past as I found my way around Melbourne relatively easily. I was proud of myself as I rarely got lost in the early days. I often used the OPSM as a landmark to guide me in the direction of La Petite. It was further up Collins Street and on the opposite side but at least when I sighted it I knew I was on the right path back to my workplace. The other prominent building on the same side as OPSM was the Reserve Bank. This building looked like it had been built without a budget as it had lots of white marble and black granite. Many people found it imposing. I also knew that the Coates building was in Collins Street. I had foolishly initially thought this building was linked to the Coates sewing threads only to discover later that the building was purchased by a grazier in the 1800s called Walter Coates. This was such a disappointment for me as I had imagined a building full of sewing treasures.

When Nell and Pat Rogers required something there was no time to spare. If I returned with the correct lining, buttons, interfacing or other requirement there was little praise but if I could not secure the necessary fabric or trimming then I was chastised in copious amounts for my ineptitude. Thankfully I was a fast learner and I quickly learnt the nuances of the rag trade or the Schmatte Business as it was termed in Flinders Lane. Flinders Lane was so well known that it was often referred to as 'the Lane' and was the centre of Melbourne's wholesale rag trade. A lot of Jewish immigrant families had set up business there. I discovered that in years gone by there were many more businesses that had a link to the rag trade, they had shop fronts but as property values increased they had been forced to the upper floors of the buildings. There were also big issues with space, deliveries and parking for customers so the rag trade was obviously declining although I thought it was still a hive of activity and a thriving industry with people, traders and shoppers rushing hither and thither through the lane.

I learnt the most favourable places to obtain items and the locality that would require the shortest amount of distance to travel. The top end of Couture Collins Street had another positive, besides being in the upper echelon of the Melbourne fashion world, it was close to shops, department stores, suppliers and of course the necessary transport to get to such places. I usually found though that foot and shoe power were the quickest and cheapest, which suited Mrs Rogers as she didn't appreciate the waste of even one single solitary cent on unnecessary items. Thankfully I did not have to run backward and forward to the button coverers, which the previous junior had been assigned to, as the tailoring department was now the proud owner of a button covering machine. I had even been allowed to use it once or twice with mixed results.

On my first day at La Petite I learnt about the dreaded time clock. The procedure was quite simple really; if you were 5 minutes late then you would be docked that time from your pay. If you worked 15 minutes overtime or arrived early for work employees did not receive extra pay. Extra time was only classed as overtime if the employer requested the staff to work extra time and this only happened when La Petite had a forthcoming fashion parade. I needed every cent of my $12.26 per week pay packet so I was always early for work. It was more advantageous to catch the early train to work than fear being docked pay if I was late.

I was enthralled by the magnificent outfits in the window and the opulence of the boutique. The window at 165 Collins Street was changed every Friday and people would gather around the shop window to see what the latest fashion creation was. Many orders were taken from the beautiful masterpiece that graced the window each week. The owners took pride in presenting something of high fashion with a new twist each and every week. If a customer wished to purchase an item from the window they would usually have to wait until the following Friday to collect it as it was very important for La Petite to collect orders from the new design that was placed in the window each week. Clients who showed interest in an item in the window, which they wanted immediately, could usually be put off by gently informing them at fitting time that it required some adjustments to give them a perfect fit.

The change room had the most magnificent modesty drapes with superb gold braided tie backs with large gold and silver tassels hanging from the underside. Everything in the boutique had a stamp of quality and glamour, this was in stark contrast to the workrooms and the conditions which were anything but glamorous and at times were more like sweat houses that exploited the workers. The rooms were not air-conditioned and therefore they were hot in summer and very cold in winter. The tailoring department in the basement had it easy in the summer but the finishing room had it easier in the winter. Like the YWCA I wondered what would happen in the case of a fire as no instructions were ever given on how to depart the building in the case of an emergency.

I was informed by my co-workers that the conditions were typical for this type of industry and that actually La Petite was a lot better than some. Flinders Lane establishments were dilapidated old buildings that sometimes housed rats that had apparently come from the wharves.

Getting to work had been a critical test for a beginner such as myself. I negotiated the busy streets of Richmond, the chaotic ticket office and the feverish train travel, where everyone seemed to be packed in like sardines as East Richmond was nearing the end of the line for a train that had come all the way from Lilydale or Belgrave. The train that I caught had stopped at all stations along the way as an express train would not stop at East Richmond as it was only two stops before Flinders Street. Despite the number of people on the train some gentlemen still managed to read a spreadsheet newspaper without missing a word. They even had the technique of turning the pages down to a fine art. One particular morning while perilously hanging on to the strap suspended from the bar that was attached to the train ceiling I saw the headlines 'Great Train Robber Skipped Town'. This was indeed exciting news and something to discuss with my work colleagues. If one wished to purchase a newspaper or a magazine there seemed to be vendors in every imaginable place spruiking their wares with much gusto.

On my arrival in the city and as I rushed through the subways under the Flinders Street station I was almost dragged along by the thousands of commuters who were on their daily mission to get to their place of employment on time. In my rush I still managed to marvel at the salmon pink tiles and the black granite that adorned the subway walls and fixtures. Something in me also found them slightly amusing as they looked like something one would put in a bathroom, but they were obviously placed there for ease of cleaning and to discourage graffiti.

At day's end returning to Flinders Street in the heart of Melbourne the station was perilous at times. At the intersection of Swanston and Flinders Street the pedestrians could cross on the walk signal in any direction. I found this frightening at first as other people on foot would bang in to each other and at times the crush meant pedestrians were knocked, pushed about or even had their feet trodden on. At first I found it difficult to tackle this intersection when keeping my eyes on the myriad of clocks above the station facade. Each clock showed the departure time for the next train on any particular line. If one caught sight of the clock on the line for the train they required and it showed a departure time in two or three minutes then all of a sudden they would quicken their pace to a jog or even faster. This caused more bumping, chaos and shouts of 'sorry'. I soon learnt how to negotiate this and more importantly to remember the relevant train departure times.

In the late 1960s Melbourne was certainly exciting for a girl like me. I had to cross at the busy intersection with Swanston Street. While waiting for the lights to signal it was safe for pedestrians to cross, I would look at the imposing looking Young and Jackson Hotel on one corner and the glorious St Pauls Cathedral on the opposite corner. As I walked along Swanston Street and turned right in to Collins Street my senses were filled with a vibrant array of energy and enthusiasm. Just walking up the hill to La Petite provided me with an air of worldly sophistication that I had not known in my life before.

It was only just over a year since Jean Shrimpton had worn a dress above the knees at the Melbourne spring carnival so there were many dresses of a shorter length on view. They looked so modern and to think the papers had said the fashion wouldn't last. Minis were here to stay, with most of the girls at the YWCA embracing the look. My friend Olivia bought a magnificent white lace dress in Block arcade that was the envy of many at the YWCA.

Most girls were chastised by Matron for the shorter and shorter look and the subsequent bare legs, but in turn those same girls ignored the reprimand. With the coat dress or tent dress so much in popularity the mini showed a lot of bare skin. Add to this the platform heel shoes and of course, the matron was not going to be impressed. Hotpants were only just starting to become popular also, but it was not advisable to wear these in full view of Matron or one's parents. They were very revealing especially if they were cut high in the legs. One had to remember that this was a time of great change in the fashion world, a time when many were experimenting and breaking from traditions.

Twiggy was a role model for many girls and they couldn't wait to get the latest weekly addition of the Women's Day or the Womens' Weekly to see the latest trend, colour or style. There was plenty of paisley, some men had wide paisley ties and many of them were wearing bell bottom pants. Even the women were embracing the paisley print in their blouses and skirts. It appeared the dowdy look had well and truly left the style conscious fashionados of Melbourne.

The previous look was so matronly although many women still wore gloves, hats and coats. Not only were the hats and gloves part of the package for the outfit but many ladies embraced an 'English Rose' complexion and therefore wanted to protect their fair skin. You could see these ladies had come in to the city as a special outing. They always said on these occasions they 'were going to town'. The women wore stockings or pantyhose.

The '60s ladies usually wore a corset when they left their house unless they were pencil thin. It was unheard of for women to be in the city in bare legs or dressed in an outfit that was remotely casual or classed as house wear. Men wore suits for these outings and often a hat. Teenagers wanted to look hip and express themselves and be different from their mothers. Some girls were even wearing Lurex and polyester which clung to the bodily shape and showed off every curve. Uncomfortable undergarments and excessive layers were becoming a thing of the past, especially for the young.

One clothing item that was slow to take on for girls were jeans. Very few females wore trousers and if they did they were more likely to be a colour, even tartan was fashionable. Trousers and in particular jeans were considered unladylike and much too masculine for the female gender. To keep one's legs warm girls often wore heavy stockings or pantyhose, often with a pattern.

I couldn't wait for the time I could look in the window, and maybe even go inside The House Of Merivale and Mr John, after all not only did they sell clothes but you could hear the latest music, buy shoes to match your outfit and even makeup that was not available in the department stores. Sometimes there was even the possibility of seeing some of the hippest looks from the hot local talents of Trent Nathan, Norma Tullo, Kenneth Pirie, and Prue Acton. Coco Chanel and Schiarparelli had always been the designers that the fashion world looked up to but new trendsetters were becoming well known. Schiaparelli started designing sportswear and swimsuits to keep up with the latest trends.

Shopping wasn't easy for many people who worked full-time which was most of the working population.

Shops were only open between 9.00am and 5.00pm Monday to Friday and on Saturday between 9.00am and 12 Noon. Shoppers constantly looked at the many clocks situated about the city; they were placed on the outside of a lot of buildings and near the exit door on the interior. A watch was often considered a luxury for many people. I had received a marcasite watch from my parents for Christmas in 1966. I was firmly informed about the importance and value of the watch, adding that I was mainly receiving it so I would be on time for any and every situation when I started work the following year. I was extremely pleased with this gift; in fact, I could barely hide my excitement.

Many girls loved to shop for bargains for their 'glory box'. Once girls were teenagers they started to accumulate items to go towards the day they would marry. They would often start the glory box themselves by sewing and embroidering household linen. Girls frequently bought items from the Myer bargain basement to add to their treasures.

I had a strong attraction to fashion magazines but on my meagre pay I was unable to buy them so begging and borrowing was the next option. Usually the magazines were a week or more, even a month, out of date but I did not mind. I loved to gaze at them while passing the newsstands at the corner of Flinders and Swanston Streets. Vogue was my favourite, as not only did it include fashion and beauty but also many articles and photographs on fashion parades all around the world. This magazine particularly appealed to girls in the 1960s as that period was known as the 'sexual revolution' and Vogue would offer feature articles discussing sexuality and contemporary fashion. Sexual liberation was challenging conventional codes of behaviour and relationships. It was opening the world for girls like me to glean information on typically forbidden subjects such as contraception, nudity, homosexuality, pornography and even legalizing abortion.

Andy Warhol was mentioned at various times in Vogue as his artistic expression was something new to the world, including his painting and his silk screening. I was fascinated by the diversity of his work and his use of colours which became known as pop art.

Although the work at La Petite was difficult and in the pecking order I found I was at the bottom of the rung, all my work colleagues treated me in a friendly and helpful manner, particularly Robyn and Jan. Apart from the business owners no one treated me any differently to those who had been a servant of the company for many, many years. In fact, the knowledge imparted to me in the early months stayed with me for the rest of my life.

On the first day I did little to hide my amazement at the array of beads and embellishments, and the quantity available in the finishing room. They were so plentiful that even if a jar of seed beads or sequins were inadvertently knocked over and the contents spilt on to the floor no one clambered to retrieve them. Crystals were not treated with such disdain though.

La Petite was renowned for its extravagant, up-market, grandiose fashion parades where invitations were highly sought after by the Melbourne high society, they were sent to all the beautiful people who were guaranteed to attend wearing stunning outfits usually designed and made previously by La Petite.

There were even fitting dummy models with customer's names on them in the finishing room.

Did some women really purchase that many high-priced handmade garments that they had their own personal dummy or mannequin?

While Neil and Pat Rogers were short in stature they were impressive big shots in the world of fashion. They were often the leaders in couture and design, but it was difficult for others to follow as the Rogers spent some time each year overseas and therefore were always one season ahead. They were highly acclaimed and celebrated in the industry.

I was a tiny girl coming from a family of humans that were not at the forefront of the line that delegated one's eventual height. Even in her heeled shoes Mrs Rogers did not reach up to my height, but she was still an imposing figure. She would often stand on a wooden box, to give her added height, and then her staff would place padded items with girdle like attachments around her body, depending on who the intended client was, to give the required shape for fitting. She liked to carry out this task to establish the shape, the feel, the movement and the design of the particular garment. Attention to detail was the reason many of her clients continued to return time and again. Pat Rogers was not averse to wearing a large padded 'stomach' around her waist to imitate pregnancy. There were several in varying sizes. She was of the opinion that even in pregnancy a woman should look elegant and be able to follow the latest fashion trend. She suggested garments of modest appearance and ever the businesswoman she knew these expectant ladies would return time and time again during their pregnancy for new outfits as they outgrew ones previously made.

It was a cutthroat world being in the rag trade. The unpleasant comments about others in the industry were not shielded from the girls in the finishing room. Behind all the hype it was tough. To the outside world it was glamorous but not so in those sewing rooms.

I reminded myself regularly that I was one of the fortunate ones as the machinists had it a lot worse than me. I was being trained as a finisher which included the application of the lace appliqué, embroidery, the inclusion of all the exquisite trims and the beading of the evening gowns. I worked on many magnificent gowns and knew in my heart that I was at the superior end of the whole project and its finished splendour.

Photographers were always present at the fashion parades and the following days papers were saturated with items from the previous night's most elegant creations.

If the girls from La Petite thought they were busy before the parade ensuring each garment was completed perfectly and on time, this was nothing compared to the workload after the quarterly season parades.

Each attendee at the parade was given a small program list detailing all the items to

be shown, it was printed in gold lettering with a gold pencil attached with a gold cord and tassel. The attendees then indicated which items they showed interest in having created to fit their specific measurements. Even though there was plenty of paisley, lurex and polyester in the marketplace, the Rogers refused to embrace them insisting on only using the finest high-quality fabrics. One issue they did succumb to was the dress knee length. If a client wanted a shorter dress then their wish was granted although some of the older staff members thought some of their more mature customers looked ridiculous with a hem length above the knee. They considered that the shorter hem length lowered the class of the clients.

The clients that purchased garments from La Petite were all well-known figures in high society in Melbourne and, in fact, all parts of Australia. The wife of the Governor General, the wives of many of the state Governors, politician's wives and company executives all visited La Petite and usually walked away having placed an order for more than one garment. Many times, unrealistic finishing times were placed on the staff for a client who had not had the good sense to put their organisational skills in to action and visit La Petite much earlier. Very few high society ladies liked to be seen in garments that they had previously worn to a gala event.

Unrealistic finish dates were given by staff particularly the Rogers, who understandably, did not want to lose a sale. Pressure was put on the employees to finish garments which inevitably caused a lot of tension and bickering. Workers were quick to blame others when garments could not be completed on time when the responsibility lay solely at the feet of the first point of customer contact. Add to this fabric or embellishment shortages and it was a melting pot for internal strife and squabbling. Despite all these issues the garments seemed to eventually be completed and all the workers prepared for the ensuing influx of orders following the next parade.

Another time of the year when there was even more strain than after the parades was the period leading up to Melbourne Cup day in November. Many women seemed to leave their decisions too late. There was also the issue of Melbourne's unpredictable inclement weather, so most clients had two garments made, one for a sunny spring day and one for a chilly unseasonal day. These outfits had to be coordinated with the milliner, so selections were paramount to ensure coordination of the overall effect.

There was the inevitable fashion on the field competition and if La Petite could manage to have one of its clients win that award it would create another influx of orders. Most women also attended ladies day, Oaks Day, and naturally they wanted an outfit that was completely different to the one worn on Melbourne Cup day. In 1967 ladies continued the trend set two years ago by Jean Shrimpton, some not wearing stockings, gloves or even a hat. La Petite did not follow this trend. It appeared that the youth were trying to drive the fashion style and break with the niceties of previous eras.

I learnt from some of the long term machinists that during World War II, in fact for nearly two and a half years La Petite made the blouses for the WAAF. The Government had insisted on this as fashion houses were superfluous to the needs of the country during the war.

My mother would travel the long distance from Upper Beaconsfield to Melbourne city by bus and train every month to visit me. She would take me for lunch at the Wild Cherry in Collins Street only six doors down the hill from La Petite. This lunch outing was a luxury for us and must have been very expensive for my mother, and an impost on her budget but we both knew how much each of us looked forward to this piece of delicious extravagance. I always ordered roast lamb from the menu as it was my favourite meal. After each visit I planned to change my selection, but despite my best intentions when next visiting the Wild Cherry it never happened. My mother knew how much I enjoyed lamb and so it was always on the menu when I went home for the weekend. It was a bit of a luxury for this to happen, but my mother always managed it.

On one of her visits to the city my mother bought me

a gift. She knew that I did not have a good functioning umbrella but what she presented to me would have been better suited to the clients at La Petite. When I saw this creation, I was shocked inside and mortified but outwardly tried to show my pleasure. The magnificent handle was covered with beautiful jewels and must have cost my mother a small fortune, but to me it was an embarrassment and something I did not wish to share with my work colleagues or the other girls at the Y. I very rarely used it, my embarrassment was so great, but in the years to come I regretted the fact that I got rid of it. It was an item that came into my life much too early due to a lack of appreciation of fine accessories because of my young teenage years.

On one occasion, and one only, my mother broke with tradition and took me to Pelligrinis Espresso Bar in Bourke Street. They had imported the first espresso machine, and everybody was crazy for the coffee there. It was such a great little cafe with coffee of the like that I had never experienced before. Sadly, I was never to return there with my mother.

7

CONSTRAINED RELATIONSHIPS

Doery House was like a rabbit warren, there were corridors and different floor levels everywhere, steps up, steps down, halls running left, halls running right.

I was too frightened to venture down some of the hallways as I feared I would never find my way out. It was an unwritten law that girls were not supposed to go to any sections or wings other than the one where their bedroom was situated.

If there was a fire one didn't dare to think what would happen.

How could they cram so many rooms and people into such a small area?

While the building with its imposing frontage at the outside made it appear larger it was surely not meant to house this many people, in fact once one started to investigate the layout and venture outside the areas closest to your bedroom it became more unbelievable that so many girls resided at 353 Church Street. Maybe this was the reason there were no power points in the rooms.

The aim appeared to be to extract as much money from the greatest number of people while using the smallest amount of space.

But if there had been an accident in the downstairs kitchen there would have been little chance of anyone escaping, particularly on the upper floors or those that resided at the back of the building, there would have been a possibility that all the girls would have been incinerated. There were no fire drills, no escape plans, no emergency exits and not a fire extinguisher or fire hose in sight.

The fire escape doors were locked so I did not know how one would escape if there actually was a fire. I was to learn later that there were approximately 88 rooms of accommodation. This in itself was so frightening as many rooms had more than one occupant. If fire should break out it would be a disaster as how would all those girls be located and accounted for. It wasn't even known at any particular time who was home and who was out.

These matters were all far from the minds of all the girls who came from far and wide to reside at the YWCA.

There were many hairdressers at the Y; all had come to the city to attend Hairdressing College. I had no time for such matters as my long flowing light brown hair was one of my better attributes. I was also very fortunate to have very small ears which unlike a lot of the girls were not pierced. God had graced me with almost perfect lips in shape and definition. He had also given me almond shaped eyes of green colour with long eye lashes. I never left the Y without mascara to make those lashes look even longer than they were.

Unfortunately, this is where it all stopped as far as I was concerned. I am only five feet two inches tall with extremely fair skin and what I considered was a plain face, neither attractive nor unattractive. I was also a chronic asthmatic so all participation in sport was out which did not endear me to the opposite sex.

My fair skin had proved to be my nemesis as I had tried all my teenage years to have a tanned look. I had even gone to extremes in coating myself with a mixture of vinegar and olive oil then lying in the sun for hours. This was tantamount to roasting a chicken. This had caused a lot of pain at the time and even though I looked good for a few days I was to ascertain as the years passed that I had done irreparable damage to my skin that could not be reversed.

Thankfully as I got to my late teens my features changed and I appeared to blossom.

The fact that I could not participate in sport did not dampen my enthusiasm for Australian Rules football, and like all Victorians I was devoted to my team. I had never seen my beloved South Melbourne in a final let alone a grand final, but I continued to support them even if I was not able to attend each week. The ticket prices were not expensive but for me everything was expensive. I later went on to also become a fan of South's feeder VFA club, Port Melbourne. Like most other Port Melbourne supporters my idol was the legendary full-forward Fred Cook. It was worth the admittance price just to see him play on the forward line each week.

Those living in Richmond were football tragics and a large percentage of the residents supported the local team, in fact if you lived in Richmond but did not support Richmond VFL then you were looked on as being somewhat of a traitor. But no matter what team you supported during the winter months talk of the football consumed much of the conversation at work and at home. The most important thing in the social life to many was the footy. It was said that men could possibly give up their cigarettes or beer, but they could and would not give up their beloved Tigers.

The priest at St. Ignatius Catholic Church in Church Street said prayers for the Tigers at each service held. Women were just as fanatical about the football in Victoria as the men were. In fact, a lot of the elderly women could be seen sitting in the same seats week after week with their knitting in hand. The weather in Melbourne was unpredictable in winter and very few seats were under cover with protection from the wind and rain, hence it was common to see patrons with a thermos in hand, often filled with hot soup to help ward off the seasonal chills. The umpires were often blamed for the outcome of many games, and in fact had to be protected from the crowds. Working class feeder clubs tried to supply tough, skilled and fearless recruits to the selection panels of the VFL clubs. The same was true of most of the schools. There was prestige in having one of your charges recruited. Very few people were members of a club as it was considered a luxury and beyond the realms of the average working-class person. Being the member of a VFL club could turn a person instantly in to a respected somebody and was the only way to achieve some benefits from your club.

Being a fan of a football team brought with it strong loyalty to that club. If a person changed teams they were often looked on as a traitor. Many children wanted to switch allegiance when the club they supported continually lost matches and floundered on the bottom of the football ladder year after year.

During the depression many team members were seen as distressed men with many of the players in the reserves staying on long after they should have retired from football. They pushed themselves as for countless families the football payment, no matter how small, was the only wage they had.

Many people still residing in Richmond talked of Jack Dyer's milk bar that had been in Church Street, Richmond. Jack Dyer was Richmond's most famous VFL player and was affectionately known as Captain Blood. He played for nineteen years and many people worshipped him like a God. He had even gone to De La Salle College to improve his football brain rather than his academic brain. Many people throughout the area were still bitter and angry that the National Trust had not preserved the building and that piece of history. Another long-term Richmond player, Tom Hafey had also owned a milk bar which was very popular as it had a pinball machine. The stories abounded that the Richmond players used to go to Kanis's café in Bridge Road to eat and sometimes they even selected the team for the following game in the back room of the café.

After leaving the YWCA I was to go on and date a South Melbourne footballer. He was a talented footballer who also just happened to be extremely handsome. He went on to coach later and proved to be equally gifted. While I was infatuated with him and we had some great times often with other South Melbourne footballers and their girlfriends I soon realized that he was mostly only dating me for the sex, after all he had another girlfriend who was a Catholic like himself. He and his family would not have heard of him marrying a Protestant, after all it was not the done thing. I also knew that my family frowned on any girl of the Protestant faith marrying a Catholic. Many a family disowned and disinherited their child if they married a person from the opposite faith. Protestants looked down on Catholics although I had no idea why they always felt superior. So, I never stood a chance. I had to admit later that I was more in lust than in love and also the prestige of dating a footballer was worth the inevitable heartache and pending break-up. It was good while it lasted.

It became pretty obvious not long after arriving at the Y that plenty of the girls had left behind a boyfriend to make the trip to the 'big smoke' and their chance at a career. This was not the case for me. At the country town where I grew up I thought I had been madly in love with John Cooper and despite the fact that I was very close to his sister, Judy, he showed scant interest in me although there had been a couple of dates of sorts and a few stolen kisses. I was Judy's godmother, but even that intervention of God didn't help my case with John.

Then there was Scott Rowlans. Once again my undivided attention meant little in my quest for love. So hence I arrived at Doery House loveless.

It was obvious very early that the phones at the Y were in big demand. They had to manage with the two antiquated pay phones. They were really just like two phone boxes, the sort that were prevalent in the streets of Melbourne and suburbs. The only difference being they were inside this old YWCA building and there were no doors on the fronts of the timber surrounds that housed the phones. If a resident wanted a very personal phone conversation they knew that this was virtually impossible. If one spoke too softly to the person on the other end of the line then they could not be heard. If one spoke too loudly then all those in the vicinity of the telephone were privy to the information.

There was one other important difference in that only one made outgoing calls, but both could accept incoming calls. On my second day in residence I discovered that it was perilous to walk past the phones as I would have to answer the phone if it was ringing. I would then have to use the buzzer if the required resident lived upstairs. Of course, this all happened on the premise that someone upstairs would actually respond to the buzzer. No response meant that I had to go searching for the phone call recipient, either way, upstairs or downstairs. This happened to all the girls and so unless you were expecting a call you made it your intention to avoid the phone area at all costs.

The girls weren't supposed to yell or run at the Y but every evening you could hear girls calling other resident's names mostly in the fruitless search for someone's loved one. I often wondered why everybody became invisible when there was a call for them.

I learnt early on in my time at the Y to stay away from the phone area unless I wanted to spend my time yelling and running, and subsequently then being yelled at by Matron. I had been instructed, by my mother, that if I wished to contact them then I should ring home and reverse the charges. This was a slightly complicated procedure as one had to place the reverse charge trunk call with an operator who would first speak to my family asking them to authorise the payment and accept the reverse charge call from me. I was aware of my financial situation so this was preferable to having to find the money which had to be fed in to the pay phone every 3 minutes or the call would drop out and the phone line would go dead. My budget was so tight that I accepted this way of communicating with my family as quite normal. Most girls preferred that the cost of the call was incurred by their love interest or family member.

It cost five cents per call just to make a local connection so the calls to areas outside Melbourne were prohibitive. This five cents did not seem like a large amount but it was not an insignificant amount as living at the Y was not exactly bargain basement rental, in fact for what one received it seemed that looking after the country girls also extended to keeping them penniless.

It was around this time that I noticed Olivia. I became aware that Olivia, along with so many other girls spent long periods around the phone area waiting for phone calls from their boyfriends. Olivia was constantly asking all who were on the telephone how long they would be on their call. She always had a frustrated and impatient look on her face which seemed to increase with every passing minute. It was more disturbing for her when girls would eventually finish their call only to have the phone ring immediately after they had replaced the receiver to find the call was not for Olivia and she would have to wait another ten minutes or more for her anticipated call. Her loud voice and requests were interminable. Every night she appeared to be at the small wooden recess that housed the phones. Most of the girls, like me found it highly amusing to hear her screaming out about the need to keep the phone lines open as she was waiting for a treasured call and it was obvious to all that she considered herself to be in love. Sometimes she went to bed without the long-expected call as James had probably given up after finding the lines to the Y were constantly engaged.

James came from Foster in Gippsland, Victoria and was Olivia's devoted love. The great problem was that numerous other girls 'were in love' and needed the phone at any cost and at the same time as Olivia.

The other amusing aspect of this nightly ritual was

that once the said lover was on the other end of the line, no one but no one, could get the recipient of the call off the line despite there being a strict rule about ten minute phone calls which no one seemed to take any notice of, especially Olivia.

Matron would do the rounds but not too many girls would give up or dob on a phone user as after all one ever knew when you would need an extended phone call yourself.

Over the coming months I began to wonder how I could actually get a boyfriend as I had slowly picked up whispers of horror stories from girls who had finally ensnared a male but had just as quickly seen them disappear in to the sunset once they realised they could not get into the said girl's bedroom, and even if they could get into the hostel as a visitor and in to the frigid sitting room, they were made to feel like a contagious disease by Matron. No male of sound mind would enter the sitting room anyway as it was the most unromantic love killing room in the universe. The other love killer was the horrendous hours that were enforced as closing times for the girls at Doery House, that is if they did actually go out in the evening. The only late closing night was Saturday and that wasn't exactly what the girls called late, but it seemed to be what the Y deemed late. Normal Saturday night closing was 12.30am and you could apply for a late pass once a month, but never on a Sunday to Thursday evening which left only Friday and Saturday. Any wonder girls went home for the weekends.

Olivia told a great story about a boy who scaled the downpipes up the side of Doery House one night. He caused a great stir. Maintenance men arrived to next day to make adjustments and to add some barbed wire to ensure no other male was tempted to repeat the adventure.

So, with all these restrictions how was I supposed to entice a guy even to like me? I knew the scenario, I was on a date at a great pub with a fantastic band, sensational atmosphere, great crowd, I look at my watch and exclaim to my date, 'oh I have to go, I have to be in by 11.00'. Wow, that would really make a guy want to date me. And heaven forbid if you were late even by one minute as you would be locked out. This made me extremely nervous as I knew not a single other living sole within a forty-kilometre radius of the hostel, let alone someone who lived around the corner.

This meant that I could not knock on their door late at night and inquire 'can I sleep on your couch'?

The YWCA had no contingency plan in an emergency so in this regard they appeared to be quite happy and relaxed in the knowledge that 15 or 16-year-old girls could be left in Church Street for the night.

With all this in mind I still had my sights set on Darryl, he lived in the city, and was the brother of Y resident Kathryn. I often saw Darryl when he brought Kathryn home. He was always well dressed, and I could see that he looked after his body. On warmer days when he was wearing a short-sleeved shirt or a t-shirt I couldn't help but notice the tanned skin and his muscular arms.

Kathryn and Darryl had come from Bendigo and Darryl lived with some mates in a flat in South Melbourne. This all seemed like a good option for me as Darryl was aware of the horrendously strict closing hours for the girls.

Darryl finally asked me out, joy oh joy. I spent what little money I had on a new skirt for the occasion, it was the latest trend of a black and white pleated skirt with a chain belt, but as the evening unfolded it turned out this was a precious resource wasted as Darryl only had one thing on his randy mind, which required as few clothes as possible. I was not giving away my virginity to him or anyone else for that matter, on a first date.

I wasn't frightened of becoming pregnant because long ago I had been given a packet of tablets by my doctor, and with the blessing of my mother, due to ongoing menstrual problems. This little packet was very clever showing which days to take which tablets, so you didn't forget. I did wonder from time to time why seven of the tablets in the little blister strips were a different colour to the other twenty-one. These monthly painful events often saw me taken to hospital while I was still attending high school.

My mother must have thought I would run off and give myself to the first boy I kissed as she did not communicate to me for many years that I was actually taking the contraceptive pill. Like many girls of the time they were not well informed on matters of the human body, they were often kept in the dark and only given facts on a need to know basis. This resulted in me being very angry after I found out the truth and an argument ensued with my mother, with me accusing her of not trusting me. Thanks to my older sister, Anne, I eventually found out why seven of the tablets were a different colour to the other twenty-one. Talk about how fortuitous it was that Anne had gone on to become an exceptional nurse, also completing her midwifery.

I had been extremely naive. Anne gave me information that would have been 'nigh on' impossible to receive from other channels, especially my mother. Anne allowed me to paw over every page of her nursing books gleaning details and facts that weren't even available to a lot of my friends. I knew my mother and father would not have been amused if they knew Anne was helping me to find out more than they would have thought appropriate. These books also had graphic pictures and diagrams of both the female and male anatomy. Things that I had never even visualised were shown with in-depth descriptions. I found that Anne would answer any and all of my questions without hesitation, and which did not cause any embarrassment to either of the sisters.

About this time, I discovered that my father had a copy of the much talked about novel 'Lady Chatterley's Lover'. I had heard it was a rich novel full of love, sex and class. Apparently it had been censored when it was originally published for being immoral. The author had already been condemned for his books 'Women in Love' and 'Sons and Lovers'. I had read 'Sons and Lovers' but how was I going to lay my hands and eyes on 'Lady Chatterley's Lover', and return it when finished? I knew the penalty would be harsh if I was discovered.

First things first though, I had to find out where my father had stashed it and this is where my sister's invaluable knowledge came in again. Anne and I were extremely close, although sadly with the passing of the years we drifted apart. Anne seemed to be able to procure anything if the will was strong enough, and for me the will was strong, after all I was the sister that was her alibi years ago when she 'wagged' school finding better things to fill her day with. When she gave 'Lady Chatterley's Lover' to me she told me to read it as fast as I could and to return it to the bottom shelf of the book case in the lounge, making sure to place it behind the large nature and travel books that were placed flat on the pine timber shelving. I was instructed to position it with the cover facing towards the back of the upright section. No wonder I had not been able to find it as none of the sisters would ever think to shift, let alone look at, the nature and travel books. All except Anne of course.

I found this book enlightening if not a tad disappointing. The hype amongst my school buddies and town friends in general had made the book sound extremely alluring and sexual but maybe this was just an overdone build up as it was unattainable to almost all in the circle of people I knew. Some of my friends wanted to borrow it from me but I could not risk the chance of being caught by my father.

And what if one of my friends lost it when it was on loan from me?

Every day I had the book and it was not in its secret location on the bookshelf weighed heavily on my mind. When I replaced the book in its hiding place I felt a bit let down by the whole experience.

Anyway, I didn't tell Darryl any of the information about the contraceptive pill and I knew I could have easily weakened in my resolve not to give myself over to him. When I saw him pull up in his Red Datsun, with Creedence Clearwater Revival blaring out from the dashboard of the car, he all of a sudden seemed very appealing. Darryl looked sexy in his bell bottom trousers and tight shirt with a paisley pattern, his hair was in a long mod style and I noticed he wore the latest Beatle boots. It turned out that he was a great Creedence fan, as I was, and the music I was hearing was coming from the cassette tape. He had a complete tape of their music and John Fogarty was belting out 'Heard it through the Grape Vine'. It was going to be a good night or so I thought. Darryl had informed me when he had asked me on a date that we would go to the new Hoyts Cinema in Bourke Street to see 'The Graduate'. I was so excited as co-workers had told me how congenial it was, but this all changed when Darryl arrived at the hostel to announce we were off to the pub. Despite my disappointment I decided at least I was about to embark on the long-anticipated date.

Things went downhill after we left the Vaucluse Pub in Swan Street, showers were starting to fall, and Darryl decided he wanted value for the money he had spent on the outing and the drinks. He didn't factor in the matter of non-compliance by the other party.

I did not comply with his persistence in the front seat of his car outside the Y, but he would not take no for an answer and subsequently he still managed to remove the erection from his trousers and try to force himself on to me. His impatience with me and the need to relieve himself quickly of the ever-swelling organ saw him ejaculate all over my new skirt. As all of this unfolded John Fogarty reached a crescendo in his song 'Have You Seen the Rain'. Good timing. Darryl was furious with me because this was not what he envisaged and likewise I was furious with him due to the fact that I thought my skirt had been ruined. He may have eventually won me over if he had dated, courted and made me feel special for more than a few hours. A trip to the see 'The Graduate' might have helped also. I never saw Darryl again, good riddance I thought, and it was some time before I could look his sister, Kathryn, in the eye when we spoke. I did not know why this occurred as I was fairly certain Darryl would not have articulated to his sister information about his failed conquest. One thing was for sure from that day forward every time I heard a Creedence Clearwater Revival song I thought of Darryl.

It was a long time before my next attempt at a boyfriend, who came in the form of a guy named Kevin. He was a dental equipment technician at the dental surgery I worked at after leaving the rag trade in late

1968. A couple of dates ensued but once we were chastised by Matron for kissing and canoodling outside the front door of the Y Kevin decided this relationship was on a highway to nowhere. I wondered if that woman had eyes in the back of her head, she seemed to be everywhere. And then there were those rules informing all the residents they were not to stand or talk to friends at the front of Doery House, let alone kiss them.

I didn't venture too much into relationships after that, I was too inexperienced, shy and introverted. I gave up, preferring to listen to the escapades of all the other girls, some of the time with much envy. Some of the girls had the most handsome boyfriends who called at the Y to collect them for a date. Lots of them were taken for picnics, the beach, for dinner or the movies. The common thread in a large percentage of these relationships was that they commenced before the girls arrived at the Y, so a loving connection had already been established which the male did not want to easily relinquish.

Not all relationships for the girls at the Y ended happily. Wendy always seemed pretty butch to me, I thought she must have been a lesbian. I actually liked Wendy a lot, and from time to time I made Wendy some nice shirts to go with her unfeminine trousers and heavy shoes. She was always great fun to be around and in the early days was most friendly picking up on the fact that I was petrified of my new life and surroundings. Wendy always talked about males in a

89

derogatory way, putting them down at any opportunity which only fuelled my opinion. I never saw her in a skirt or dress, and she never wore makeup. Her hair was always cropped short. She came from a well to do family in Malvern who had sent her to the Y so she would become 'more well-rounded'.

What did that mean?

About a year after arriving at Doery House Wendy discovered she was pregnant. This couldn't be possible as she didn't even like men. There were floods of tears and much sadness. Most of the other girls knew of her predicament but she kept it from Matron Lamrock as long as possible. She talked of an abortion but there were too many horror stories of back-yard jobs. Girls almost bled to death, some had permanent injuries, some would never have children again and there was even the occasional death. Everybody seemed to know of dodgy premises, but no one knew of anyone reputable that could be recommended.

Wendy refused to go to Dr. Roseby next door in Church Street. Wendy expounded to anyone who would listen that she should not have got pregnant as that was the first time she had ever had sex.

Why wasn't she told, why wasn't it taught at school, why wasn't it public knowledge? This was an eye opener for a lot of the girls as they also thought one couldn't get pregnant if you were a virgin when having sex for the first time. I was naïve, but thankfully not that naïve.

Wendy left Doery House not long after this revelation,

we never heard from her again, but we did learn she had adopted out her baby. One of the girls at the Y worked at a florist where a co-worker knew Wendy's mother who had conveyed this small piece of information or we would never have known. I missed Wendy very much as she was a straightforward person who had called life as it was, all of it tinged with a lot of fun. Wendy had deserved happiness back in her life.

Other relationships had also started out as a supposed journey of never-ending bliss but were to end abruptly due to the over-sexed male needing to impose himself on a young girl looking for companionship or even love.

One chilly night in the winter of 1969 a date began innocently but ended with the rape of Claire.

She had been a virgin so there was no hiding the evidence of the loss of her virginity to her friends. That blood, the dishevelled and torn clothes, the smudged mascara and the smeared lipstick all made it evident all was not well in paradise.

Matron was called and she subsequently summonsed the police. I saw the blue uniforms, heard the sobs and glimpsed the matron's horrified face.

Had Claire heard such descriptive details of the male and female bodies before and if so had she visualised this all playing out in such a brutal way?

When Claire was describing the attack, the hitting of her face and the pain to her private parts as she termed them, it all seemed too horrific. As I was prone to have nightmares the whole episode played out in my mind for months, each dream becoming more horrendous than the last.

Claire, it turned out had lived a sheltered life with her only sibling, a younger brother, in the town of Nagambie. Like me her life had been shielded from harsh and stressful times. She knew little of the matters of sexual encounters and the urgent requirements of young males with an excess of testosterone.

I was to learn that the sight of an erect penis had almost been enough to make Claire scream let alone the torture that followed on this occasion. Claire had described how her attacker had a tight grip around her throat and the other hand had covered her mouth. She had tried to bite him, but he had warned her that she would cop worse than she was already going to get if she struggled or injured him. She had felt the screams coming up in her throat, but she just could not get them to come out. She was to glean from the police that the pressure on her throat would have stopped her from crying for help. She was slight in build, with thin arms and wrists that looked like they would break with little resistance. She would have been no match for any male let alone a well-built mature virile man.

When Claire learnt from the female police officer that there was a chance of a sexually transmitted disease or even pregnancy the life seemed to drain from Claire's body.

She wanted the fellow who took her on this date to pay and nothing seemed to stop her need for revenge. Her day in court did eventually arrive after the police ultimately found the perpetrator. Claire was to learn that all is not fair and equitable in the justice system when the victim described Claire as a wanton slut, that she was a willing participant and that she made herself look like she did when she returned to the Y to place the blame on someone else should she be discovered. Nobody seemed to be interested in the black eye that developed the day after the attack or the myriad of bruises on the inside of her legs that were black, then purple, then yellow over the coming week. The culprit was found not guilty due to insufficient evidence.

How could this have happened when she thought the magistrate would be sympathetic to the victim?

Claire found it difficult to function for some months. Thankfully Dr. Roseby found she did not have a sexually transmitted disease and she was not pregnant.

During the following year Claire saw an article showing a photograph of the guy who had raped her. The headlines read 'Five Years for Rape'. Justice at last.

8

THE DRESSMAKER UNLEASHED

Life went on at the Y and slowly I settled in to a routine of sorts. Even though the living conditions were not ideal, and the food was average at best I did make some exceptional friends as time went by. Some of the girls would not become close friends and even though I was quite different to most of them with a dissimilar background, on the whole everybody was pleasant. The most notable difference for me was that the bullying I had received through my early teenage years had disappeared. I was so grateful for this. I even believed that my roommates early stealing escapades had not been done for bullying reasons but more because Ronnie did not have respect for others possessions.

As long as one abided by the strict rules at Doery House and avoided the Matron at all costs then all was well. With the camaraderie of the other girls, who were mostly good fun, one could get up to all sorts of mischief and still stay loosely within the rules.

It was obvious within a short space of time that this was no home away from home but the majority of girls made the most of the situation and stayed happy in the knowledge that the frequent visits to their family would sustain them for another week or two. Many of them got help with their finances and all of them would bring back goodies of the food variety as treats to improve the poor food that was on offer at the Y. Frequent talk consisted of the love and separation from their siblings but then all the girls managed to find 'sisters' in residence at Doery House that would ease their minds through troubled times and importantly share in the excitement of some new found happiness be it of the employment variety or the latest love interest.

Most of the girls were fearless and therefore did not concern themselves with the day to day happenings in the world including politics. Even the sad and dramatic things that occurred to some of the residents or the surroundings at the Y did not seem to deter the girls from their daily lives or participating in an upcoming event or adventure.

I decided during the loneliness and isolation I would use some of the hours after the evening meal to continue with one of my great loves and the reason I was in this dreaded place, and that of course was sewing. The hostel sewing machine was an old Singer model that had a multitude of problems not least being the bobbin thread tension. When I suggested the machine needed to be serviced, and even giving Matron the name of the repair man in Bridge Road, she looked at me incredulously and without saying a word implied that this was out of the question by dismissing me from the room. Repeated requests to anyone who would listen fell on deaf ears and so I eventually gave up, deciding that I would bring my own sewing machine from home, that is if my mother would give her permission.

My mother was not altogether happy about this request as the machine had been given to me for my fifteenth birthday and obviously the household budget was stretched for this purchase. My mother dished out strict instructions on what was expected of me in relation to the sewing machine.

And there was the matter of what was to happen when I went home at weekends, whose sewing machine was I going to use then?

This all seemed like a storm in a teacup as my mother had a sewing machine that I had used before the precious fifteenth birthday present.

Thankfully girls who had sewing machines could leave them in the office at Doery House for safe keeping; this therefore seemed to satisfy my mother that all would be well. I did not articulate to my mother that I had not seen any other sewing machines in the office at the YWCA. As with everything associated with living at the Y this was not a straightforward procedure. One had to ask permission from Matron who read the riot act about the rules and regulations and that the YWCA would not be liable for any damage or loss of the machine. 'If your machine is broken or any part of it disappears don't come crying to me young lady, and we will need to arrange a suitable time for the delivery of the machine', she bellowed in her usual brash voice. I was willing to take my chances. I was informed by the lady in the office who took care of all such matters, that the machine had to be clearly labelled with my name or it would not be looked after.

Sewing machines had figured predominantly in my life for reasons other than sewing. When I was a young teenager my older sister Anne also liked to sew, therefore the machine was in demand at certain times. I remember one particular sewing machine event when my sister Anne, younger sister Ellen and I were having an enormous argument. I was leaning towards being on the side of Ellen in this sisterly dispute. I had a closer relationship with Anne than with Ellen but that was probably because we were only sixteen months apart in age, but on this particular occasion I thought Ellen was in the right and besides Anne was having one of her 'holier than thou' days, so why would I side with her. Anne lauded over her siblings as her paternal grandparents had fostered the notion in Anne that the oldest child was always superior. At this time in my life my youngest female sibling, was still a baby and my brother had still not been born.

Anne had been working away at the sewing machine as the argument continued when all of a sudden Ellen shoved Anne's head in to the machine to keep her quiet. The thread take-up lever on the top of the machine went perilously close to Anne's eye and left a deep gash with plenty of blood running from the side of her nose. Anne leapt from the chair chasing us down the back stairs of the house. She picked up a brick and threw it at us but thankfully she was a bad shot and the brick hit the wall. Anne managed to garner the sympathy of our mother after this incident. She was left with a nasty scar which was a constant reminder to Ellen that her actions may not have been her best choice of revenge.

My Nana had an old treadle machine which was frequently in use. I remembered how much my mother's mother liked her sewing machine informing all who would listen that she would not be buying a new 'fandangle' electric sewing machine which were just glorified thread wasters.

The sewing machine supplied by the YWCA did not come with bobbins or needles, these had to be purchased separately from the office, hence this was another reason I did not want to use the outdated old clunker. I went to Matron hopeful of a positive response to my request - 'please can I have my sewing machine delivered by my father next week as he is making a trip to Melbourne'. 'Go away girl, you have caught me with more pressing matters on my mind. There is one available here for your use if required'. Surely she saw my disappointment.

Another two weeks passed by. 'Matron, my father is coming this way from our country home next week', but before I could finish the sentence I was interrupted by Matron barking at the top of her vocal range, 'Heavens above girl, cooks help hasn't turned up and you want me to be thinking about a sewing machine'.

The weeks and requests passed by. About this time, I was making my deb dress as I was to be a debutante in a few months' time. My Father was a Freemason and every year the Lodge he belonged to arranged and conducted a Debutantes ball in the winter. All girls aged 16 years and over were able to participate even if their father was not a Freemason. It was called the Pakenham Masonic Debutante Ball and was considered a significant milestone in a girl's life, particularly for a country girl. I was to be partnered by David and we were to have dancing lessons, on Sunday nights, weekly for 6 weeks prior to the big ball. I also had to make myself a long skirt for dancing practice and lessons. The fabric I chose was a viyella fabric in blue and grey paisley. It was a custom that many girls looked forward to, especially the glitz and glamour. The parents looked forward to the formality and the history of the event. It was a costly experience, but parents always welcomed the occasion. My mother had already gone through it with my older sister Anne, so I knew that the costs were high. There would be a saving on the making of the dress, but I wanted the best Chantilly lace with the best beading. Then there was the cost of the flowers, shoes, underwear, hairdo, dancing lessons, photographer, flowers, and on and on it went.

I decided to try one more time for my sewing machine.

'Matron, about my machine'. 'Rosalie this is not the time nor the place to be discussing this, the mail has just arrived, and I need to direct my attention to that'. I decided at this point that I needed to make my point more forcefully. 'Well it appears the debutante dress I am making for my debut will not be finished in time; I had been relying on being able to complete a lot of the work here in the evenings'. At last I had caught Matron's attention. 'Wait a minute Rosalie, you are to be a debutante, well in that case you may organise the delivery of the machine to the office, but do not come to me if anything goes awry'.

This proved in many ways to be the turning point for me and my relationship with Doery House and many of the girls.

The sewing/ironing room was just a bare room with timber floors, no adornments on the walls and only one long bench to place items on. There was no heating in the ironing and sewing room although it did have two precious power points and a rickety, unstable old chair to sit on. The two power points available were the only ones possible for use by the girls at Doery House. They were at a premium for ironing and sewing in the evening. Luckily not many of the girls wished to avail themselves of a sewing machine. The same could not be said for the iron as most girls wanted to look their best for their working day. Even though the irons were in poor condition and often had brown marks on the base, they were still not freely available for use. Each girl had to collect the iron from the office and sign for it on collection and then return it complete with the obligatory signature. The room was almost adjacent to the phone cubicles, so I heard all the comings and goings each evening. I also found it to be a refuge as I would stay later in that room on the nights that I had to sleep out on the verandah. The longer I was away from that dreaded outside bed the better.

In one corner of the room was a hair dryer on a stand. Girls would often wash their hair, place it in rollers, then sit under the hairdryer until they were happy they would have a few more curls or some bounce in their hair for their night out. It wasn't exactly comfortable either as the girls had to sit with their head completely upright which meant if they wanted to read they had to hold a book up right in front of their face. It wasn't possible to listen to a wireless radio or a transistor radio as the dryer sounded like a motor bike in one's ear. You also had to be careful of that hairdryer as the dials on the top of it did not always work properly or maybe it was the temperature control, as sometimes there was very little heat coming out of the drier and at other times the girls thought their scalps would be burnt due to overheating of the machine. It was possibly another fire hazard in the building.

There was a lot of suffering that went on in the quest for a nice hairdo. The dryer in the sewing and ironing room was usually reserved for special occasions. The rest of the time the girls would have to sleep in the enormous rollers they placed in their hair, some of them did it every night. Many girls still had their hair in rollers when they went to breakfast. There was a strict rule that the hair must be covered with a scarf. This rule also applied to those with an excess of pins in their hair. Girls were not allowed at any meal table with rollers or pins showing. Claire, who was a hairdresser, would style the hair of many of the girls. She was often in the sewing room at the same time as I was, and I always marvelled at the creations she could produce.

Hot rollers were starting to become popular as well, although most girls could not afford them, and there was always the problem of finding a power point to heat them. They did not perform as well as the conventional way but still those that had them were constantly fielding requests to lend their new hair rolling creation to others.

Some of the other residents would come each evening to discover what I was currently working on. They were amazed at the intricacy of my debutante dress with its heavy Chantilly lace and the delicate beading with thousands of beads, sequins and crystals.

I managed to finish the dress with the assistance of one of my co-workers from La Petite. Jan had been in the finishing room at La Petite for many years and along with Robyn they were the most experienced beaders. She was a wonderful mentor to have. She lived in Williamstown and suggested that I go to her place on several weekends so she could help with the fittings and ensure the dress was finished on time. I spent hundreds of hours working on my gown and with Jan's guidance the whole experience was worth every minute. I was amazed when it was completed at how magnificent the end result was. I went on to make my debut with my partner David.

Each debutante was given the position that they would be presented to the Masonic Lodge Grand

Master and his wife. This was allocated at random with each girl not knowing until the ballot was drawn in what position they would be presented. One of the most important tasks the girls had to complete on the night was a full curtsy to the ground when being presented to the Grand Master. The lucky boys only had to bow. I drew the last position which at first had me most disappointed. My Uncle, who was my father's brother, found out about my disappointment and decided he could rectify the matter in a spectacular way. He was in charge of the spotlight on the night of the ball and he managed to make sure the spotlight shone on me as I arrived at the top of the stairs, and followed me all the way to my curtsy and my final position, after all there was no one after me to steal the spotlight. Under that light all those crystals shone brightly for everyone at the Masonic Ball to remember.

I was to go on and make two more debutante dresses for other debs in the future. One memorable one was in white velvet with a full skirt, it was trimmed with glorious white feathers around the hem and the three-quarter sleeves.

About the time I had been pleading for the sewing machine delivery another problem had presented itself, I needed a new, clean, modern steam iron that was exclusively mine. The only solution was to buy one but where would I get the money. I needed to investigate this. For several days during my lunch break I researched irons and finally sourced the one that I felt would suit my needs best, the only drawback was that it cost $12.50, this was more than my whole weekly wage. There was nothing for it but to put the iron on lay-by and pay it off at $1.00 per week.

This meant I would not own the iron for thirteen weeks and what was I going to do in the meantime?

What could I forego; even finding $1.00 per week seemed out of the question?

But I was steadfast, I could not and would not allow one of the old YWCA irons with the frayed twisted cords and baked on burn marks on the iron soles to wreck anything I had spent hours creating. As it was, to get me through, I had been laying an old sheet between the fabric and the iron to ensure scorch marks did not appear on any of my handiwork. And nothing, but nothing would influence me to put those old irons in the proximity of my debutante dress. Two weeks later I plucked up the courage to convey the dilemma to my mother. 'Really Rosalie, there is always something more you require, but I am prepared to lend you the balance of the money you owe on the iron, you can get it out of lay-by and you can repay me the $1.00 each week'. I threw my arms around my mother. Problem solved.

Of course, there was still the predicament of the need for hot water for my hot water bottle. As I now had the precious iron sorted out the next purchase would be a 'Birko' which would boil water for the water bottle. When I did manage to purchase one I was careful Matron did not find out that I was boiling water in the ironing room as I knew what the implications would be.

Once again Wendy was a great watch out for me and in exchange Wendy could use the 'Birko' when she needed it. Many girls did discover the truth and I became popular with many of the other Doery House residents who had hot water bottles. They were a popular commodity on the cold winter nights in the chilly beds at the Y. I decided that if someone wanted hot water they had to be in the ironing room with me at the same time so I could supervise. I would not lend my mini kettle to anyone under any circumstances with the small exception of Shirley and Olivia who had become my trusted friends.

Generally, the girls at the Y were very careless with others possessions and as I had worked so hard and for so long for the items I had I was not about to allow others to destroy my belongings. This attitude was not endearing to some of the other occupants, but I had made up my mind and would not digress from my principles.

At the same time as I was making my deb dress I was putting together a floral yellow sun dress. This caught the eye of many an admirer and requests came from other girls to make them garments. I saw an opportunity to make a little money and possibly repay my mother quicker than she anticipated. I was always diligent in repaying my debts as I knew if further money was required in the future then I had a better chance of receiving it.

I charged $2.00 per garment and $3.00 if it had trimmings. Kathy came to me first with a request. As I could not as yet draft patterns the girls had to use the patterns I had available or a new pattern would need to be purchased. Fabric had to be chosen along with trimmings, so we went shopping for suitable fabric, ribbon, zipper colour, buttons, hooks and eyes, thread and lining colour. This was so much fun for me and I could feel life would be a little bit different from now on. I enjoyed shopping with the girls and the discussions over the design and the fabric.

The girls always stood on the bench in the ironing/sewing room to have the hem length measured, which was always above the knee. This trend had not waned at all as some fashion experts had suggested. For this task I needed to engage a person as a lookout, because if Matron found out I was encouraging anyone to stand on the precious YWCA bench then I knew it would be the end of the sewing privileges. Wendy was usually only too happy to carry out this task and she was diligent and enjoyed being wanted by the other girls. She had a secret little code or word to signal to me when danger was approaching. Much to the relief of all involved we were never caught, although it is a wonder our antics were not exposed as over the months and years one end of the bench appeared to be slowly coming away from the wall probably from the weight of girls continually standing on it. It was most surprising that the despicable act of standing on the bench was not discovered, as the girls often commented that there was no need for a closed circuit TV at the Y as they felt Miss Lamrock was one and the same thing. It was almost impossible to get away with anything.

The night Kathy modelled the completed red and white dress in the television room I knew I would never be bored or lonely at Doery House again. Girls started to arrive on most nights with requests for the latest fashion to be made up for them in their size.

I would grant most wishes, but some were beyond me mainly because of the time constraints. Some girls would appear in the sewing room on a Tuesday or Wednesday evening requesting a new dress for the following Saturday night. This was totally unrealistic in my eyes as I would already have several projects in progress.

Girls wanted bell-bottom pants, culottes and box-shaped dresses. Some brought me psychedelic prints or tie-dyed fabric that had been created in the bath at their home. Tie-dyed fabric was the rage for those who liked flowing dresses like caftans or ankle length culottes. I even made a pair of white knee length culottes for a girl who was in the Victorian Women's cricket team.

The girls at the Y wanted to show their favouritism for Mods, Rockers, Bodgies or Widgies in the clothes they wore. They also wanted to have their clothes modelled on the London Carnaby Street fashion. I certainly had to be versatile and at times found it difficult to keep up with all the new trends. At times it seemed like 'anything goes'.

Boots were definitely in style so often the girls wanted

a mini skirt to match designed with a hemline that was at least three inches above the knee, and the skirt fabric had to match their bright knee-high boots. Shift dresses, fluorescent colours and shiny fabrics with mismatched patterns sporting large buttons were all in fashion and thankfully very easy for me to sew and finish quickly. Some of the outfits called for transparent sleeves. I disliked animal prints but in 1969 this became very popular particularly in miniskirts. A lot of the girls liked shift dresses with 'Peter Pan' collars. This style of dress was considered a great new fashion as one could get rid of the dreaded corset.

The girls were wearing stilettos to work so they often brought these to me to see if I could find a suitable matching or complementary fabric.

Jeans were also becoming more and more popular but mercifully Levi Strauss, Wrangler and Lee Rider took care of this hot new item for girls. Some girls even preferred their jeans frayed so they looked like hippies, they teamed these with leather sandals. My mother had informed me in the past that jeans should not be worn by girls as they were not ladylike for females and they were just a sign of youth rebellion. They were still not accepted at one's employment or the theatre or restaurants, but they were slowly becoming a casual wear fashion staple, particularly if worn with a T-shirt. Even though my mother considered not only jeans but all trousers for women were masculine and consequently forbade her daughters wearing them, there was just no stopping fashion. Slowly but surely trousers, including jeans became popular due to their comfort, versatility and durability. Women could dress them up or down, casual or smart, with jackets or sweaters. The leg could be any length, close fitting or baggy. Girls felt that by wearing trousers they were showing their equality to men. Drainpipe jeans as worn by members of the band, The Rolling Stones, also became popular for girls and boys alike.

At the same time girls were becoming more daring with their hosiery with tights of various colours becoming popular in the winter months. At first sight of seeing me wearing black thick tights my father called me 'liquorice legs'.

While sewing I would listen to my favourite music, from my small transistor radio, which included the Rolling Stones, The Who, Creedence Clear Water Revival, Rod Stewart and the Small Faces and The Kinks.

For evening wear, I was asked to make a mini cocktail dress for June, the sleeves were of a wide trumpet shape and were made of maroon chiffon while the dress was of a velvet fabric. I had a dreadful time getting the welt to run all in the one direction but when it was completed there were lots of favourable comments at the final fitting. June did not want to wear a corset as she said they were too constricting and besides it was obvious when wearing the dress. She wore patent leather stilettos and carried a patent leather bag with the dress. She had her hair in a cropped style which was becoming all the rage thanks to the model Twiggy.

When her boyfriend arrived to collect her, he was wearing a grey suit with bell bottom trousers and pointy toed beetle boots. What a great looking couple they made.

I longed to be able to design and draw my own patterns but alas I could make alterations to a bought paper pattern, but I was unable to create my own designs and transfer those to paper. I made it my goal to remedy that situation.

I was to go to a dinner dance in the city with my parents, my oldest sister, Anne, and two guys from my hometown in the country. This was to be a special event, so I decided to make a two-piece hot pink outfit in crepe fabric. Crepe was not an easy fabric to work with, but the finished results were usually stunning. The top had long sleeves with a peter pan collar. The front had beaded buttons and the pants were floor length flowing culottes. I beaded a wide section around the sleeve cuffs and the bottom of the pants in crystals, seed beads and sequins in cream shades. The outfit took many, many weeks to complete. Each evening in the sewing room at the Y the girls would call in to see how the outfit was progressing and when it was completed they were in awe of the results. The evening was a great success as it was a special event for my mother and father. One of their favourite artists were Jackie Trent and Tony Hatch and on this night they sang their favourite song "Just the Two of Us".

I tried to get fabric from Balls on the corner of Church

and Swan Street but regrettably they often didn't have the variety of fabric or the right adornments. This often meant that my 'customer' would have to purchase the items elsewhere and this often meant a trip to the city to Clegs.

Balls was an enormous building with creaking wooden floors. They had roll upon roll of fabric along with all manner of sewing items, accessories, haberdashery and even manchester. Unfortunately, the place was very dusty and always looked in disarray. The sales assistants always seemed to know where everything was located despite the place looking chaotic. It appeared items were placed at random wherever they fell but apparently this was not the case. Goodness knows when and if it was ever cleaned. The large fascination when visiting was the way they completed their money transactions. A customer would take the items they wished to purchase to the counter. The sales assistant, often a male, would write up a detailed docket from his carbon duplicate docket book, then take the customers money, then roll it inside two copies of the docket ready to be placed in a large canister above his head. The assistant would take the canister from the cradle attached to the cable holding it, then unscrew the lid, place the docket and the money inside, replace the lid and reposition it in the cradle. A lever would be pulled, and the canister would whirr up the metal cable on the track to the cashier who was situated out of sight. The cashier must have checked all the details, then replaced one copy of the docket and the change in the canister before sending it buzzing back to the salesperson to give to the customer. The sales person would then tear brown paper from an extremely large paper roll holder on legs, wrap the purchased articles, tie it up with string or twine, making a loop at the end for the customer to use as a handle for carrying home. This whole procedure was worth the visit alone but not if you were in a hurry as the entire process took many minutes to complete.

Balls closed sharply at twelve noon on a Saturday, the only day available to shop if I wanted to go with my 'customer'. This meant that I could not make my usual weekend trip home to my family but if it meant I got the right items and I could spend the weekend sewing then this was tolerable. Sometimes when I thought of hunting for fabric and a new sewing project it drew me in like a drug and had a greater pull than the trip to my hometown. I always made my 'customer' check Balls first as I did not want to waste time going there and discovering the visit was a waste of time and that I had foregone my weekend visit to my family.

If we arrived too close to Balls twelve noon closing time we would not be served, as customers had to be out of the shop by twelve noon sharp. One such day June and I arrived ten minutes before closing and devised a way to get the necessary shopping done. June already knew the fabric she wanted, having checked it out the week before, so upon entering the store she grabbed the roll and I proceeded to the counter. After the fabric was measured I reminded the

112

salesman not to forget the thread, zipper and hooks and eyes I had placed under the roll. As he looked for them and insisted they weren't there a heated discussion took place with me averring he must have dropped them. The salesman did not want to lose our custom and after all he had already cut the measured fabric, so he had to allow us to get the substitutes for the so-called misplaced items. We left the store at ten minutes past twelve listening to the manager chastising the salesman for allowing them to run late, 'it is not good enough, this will not happen in the future, instead of being paid extra you will be docked ten minutes from your Saturday pay'. Goodness what a fuss over such a small matter but I decided it would be wise not to try that stunt again.

9

TWO HOMES

The journey home each weekend was mixed with so many emotions. I disliked living at the YWCA, but I did not always rejoice in my trips home on Friday evenings.

Homesickness is a terrible affliction; it made me depressed, lonely, and melancholy, and particularly miss the things in my life that had never been of importance before. It would produce tears at the most inappropriate times. At times I felt like I was still a child who could not manage without my mother and yet I was suddenly thrown in to an adult world, where I had to survive at all costs. I knew that some of the things I undertook in my daily life were not appropriate for a girl of my age but there were no alternatives. The girls around me pulled me along in their own wave of survival and before long I felt like I was able to stand tall and conquer the world.

The trips home were something that were looked forward to in the early days at the YWCA but as I became more friendly with some of the girls especially Shirley I was sometimes reluctant to venture home, nevertheless these weekly visits were expected in more ways than one.

My mother particularly wanted to nurture me and

check on my well-being while my father wanted me to work in the office of the family business on Saturday mornings. I disliked this immensely as my father's business had several petrol bowsers in front of the offices. All the country folk would call at the petrol pumps for fuel on Saturday mornings and I was expected to serve them. This was usually okay but when they wanted their oil checked or their windscreen cleaned this was a matter to cause serious anxiety.

There were so many models of cars, utilities and trucks that I was petrified I would do the wrong thing and why should a girl of 15 be expected to check the oil in a customer's vehicle?

When it was established that oil was required there was the next daunting step of trying to ascertain which type of oil was required. There were so many different types and I often had to ask the assistance of the vehicle owner. Regularly if the driver was a female they did not have a clue which oil was required either.

This whole experience was torture for me, but I had to suffer in silence as I desperately wanted the pay that was offered by my father, the amount of $5.00 for 3 hours was considered a generous amount. I felt a commitment to my father; hence I went home most weekends to carry out my duty. I even went home if my parents were away which was particularly lonely. I would often have to do this if I was making an article of clothing for someone in my hometown and a fitting was required. If I was unable to venture home it was expected I would give my parents plenty of notice and

I was told by my father, in no uncertain words, that I was not to make a habit of it. My home was usually preferable to the loneliness of the YWCA on weekends. Most girls left Doery House on the weekend as it was not a place to spend available free time. I knew I should feel grateful as some girls who lived interstate did not have the option of where they would spend their weekend.

I would haul my small suitcase or bag to work each Friday. The size of the bag I took with me depended on the size and volume of sewing I was working on. I would go directly from work to the train station for my trip home. My mother would meet me at Beaconsfield railway station to take me on the 20-minute drive to our home.

As much as I enjoyed most of my weekend time at home the return trip to Doery House was an ordeal that at times terrified me. As Sunday afternoon approached I would find a deep depression clouding over me. I disliked immensely the arduous, long, dark trip back to Richmond and the thought of another harrowing week in that musty, dank, unfriendly place that was my second home.

Part of my father's duty as the owner of the trucking business was his contract with the PMG (Post Master General). This involved collecting the mail from the red mailbox in the centre of town at the front of the post office. The mail was encased in a thick canvas bag that was removed from the interior of the mailbox and replaced with a fresh one for the next day's mail. The bag was tied at the top ready to take to the Gippsland to Melbourne red rattler train. The town we lived in was at the top of a steep hill.

On the way down the hill we passed through the town of Guys Hill where the mail collection process was repeated at the post box.

Just before we reached the station there was one more box to clear. This process from home to the train took approximately 30 minutes. The train departed from Beaconsfield railway station at 8.00pm to the city. I went with my father each Sunday night.

I would hold back the tears from my father, an unemotional man, who was more interested in ensuring that the mail 'got through' and that he had accomplished his weekly Sunday evening job. After all he was of the opinion that I was not wholly his responsibility anymore, although in years to come this would all change particularly in his last weeks of life when he knew the end was almost nigh, he told several people who were aware of the way some family members had treated me 'take care of Rosalie'.

This was a terribly lonely and unhappy time each week, but I also felt that staying at the YWCA each weekend would be far worse. My mood would not be helped by the emotional farewell between my mother and me each Sunday night. My mother always gave me $5.00 on Sunday for the taxi from Flinders Street railway station to the YWCA in Church Street, Richmond. The taxi fare was usually around $4.50 and I would spend the entire trip to Doery House watching the fare metre, as I was extremely worried that the fare would actually be more than the $5.00 my mother had laid in my hand as we parted. I sometimes decided, without informing my mother, to save the money and risk catching the train from Flinders Street to East Richmond station. The taxi was faster and more comfortable, and on top of this I was tired, and it was well after 9.30pm by the time I got back to Doery House. I always took the taxi if it was raining or extremely cold.

I knew my decision not to catch the taxi was extremely foolish, as I was barely 16, of slight build and carrying a suitcase, which, when all were combined, gave lots of messages to a would-be perpetrator. On numerous occasions I took the risk in my quest to save money for something more worthwhile than a taxi ride. Each week every cent was accounted for and even 10 cents could make a difference to my life. Taking the train to East Richmond had other causes for anxiety, the weight of the case, the climb up Church Street when my tiredness was overwhelming, all those dark houses, all those Greek men sitting on their verandahs playing cards making lewd comments and all those hidden shrubs.

Which option had the greater risk?

The choice was to prove harrowing one night in the winter of 1968.

I had just crossed Swan Street and was slowly climbing the Church Street hill when from out behind a high brick fence a large, unshaven, smelly, dishevelled man jumped in my direction.

I screamed with a pitch that should have alerted most of Richmond that I was in danger. I was grabbed from behind and felt the weight of the thug around my shoulders and neck.

All my senses were heightened with the body odour, the rough scaly hands, the unshaven face and the sound of the heavy boots, along with his overpowering height.

Was I going to be raped, was I going to die, were my possessions going to be stolen?

My scream had not alerted anyone, so without outside help I knew I had to do something to rid myself of the perpetrator.

Should I leave my suitcase on the footpath and run?

With all the strength I could muster I stomped on the grubby man's foot. He yelled in pain and anger and was forced to drop his hands from my shoulders. I turned towards him and it was confirmed that my 5-foot 2-inch height was no match for this disgusting excuse for a human being. The smell of cigarettes and alcohol nearly overpowered me, but I managed to lift my right leg up with tremendous force and knee the villain between the legs.

I then turned and took off up the hill, with no concern at all for the fact that I knew running could bring on an asthma attack. The man was moaning and crying out 'you little vixen, you are going to pay for this'. I ran with a speed I did not realise I was capable of. If only I was not weighed down by the suitcase, I was sorely tempted to abandon it but thoughts flashed through my mind of the items within that were so precious to me, not least of all the fruit cake that my mother had made me to help ease the distress of not having any decent home cooking.

I could hear the thump of the man's feet on the footpath behind me. They appeared to be getting closer and closer, and what was worse was that my lungs were screaming 'stop'. I knew that very little air was getting to my lungs and it felt like my legs were going up and down in the one spot. The noise on the concrete path was getting louder and louder so I knew the man was making ground on me.

Doery house was getting closer and closer as the weight of the suitcase increased with every step. I knew I was having an asthma attack as I finally pushed the white wrought iron gate open and dragged myself down the concrete path on to the verandah. I pushed the front door open and collapsed.

I did not know how many people rushed to my aid or how I made it in to bed or who helped me with my medication.

Miss Lamrock called me to her office the next morning and despite the fact that I was still feeling quite unwell, I was informed that I must have brought it upon myself, and that I should be more careful when wandering the streets of Richmond. YWCA meant Young Women's Christian Association but sometimes I thought the 'Christian' bit seemed to have evaporated from the people who ran the facility.

Nevertheless, it was over 12 months before I caught the train again between Flinders Street and East Richmond after the sun had gone down.

I never ever disclosed to my parents the details of that night in the winter of 1968 as they had always believed that I caught a taxi from the city to the Y on Sunday nights.

10

A CALMING FRIEND

I had slowly built up some firm friendships at Doery House. This had been an extremely slow process for me as I did not make friends easily and was not one to start conversations of my own volition. I was happy for someone else to embark on a discussion and for me to join in when there was a silent moment, but other than that I preferred to listen and stay involved that way. I had arrived in early 1967 and I spent most of that first year feeling extremely alone and unhappy. Shirley arrived in early 1968 and it did not take long for us to bond, then in late 1968 Olivia arrived, and a threesome was formed.

When Shirley invited me, in mid-1968, to share a room with her I could barely contain my elation. It was a large room with two single beds in the one room, the wardrobes and dressing tables were of a better quality with a rug on the timber floor beside each bed which appeared to be in superior condition to my previous room. There was still only one single light bulb hanging from the ceiling and no power points. I could not believe I would finally be rid of the inside / outside living arrangement. Of course, naturally the board would be much higher, but I would make it work no matter how many sacrifices I had to make.

Naturally some transitions in life are not as simple as they first appear. This was not the case for Shirley and me as we were ready, willing and able from the minute we discussed this proposition. Convincing the Matron was not as straightforward. She informed Shirley that this would be a backward step for her and that she should take more time to consider the proposed action. Shirley was not at all happy with the way Matron had referred to me, as Shirley had been to my home in the country and had stayed with my family. She had found them to be welcoming and caring, and it was obvious to her that I had received a strict upbringing in a religious household.

Miss Lamrock's attitude made Shirley and I all the more determined to ensure we would room together, and so we did. Within two weeks we were in a larger double share room happily chatting until all hours every night. We eventually reduced this as we were getting so little sleep. I was so glad to be rid of my fortnightly stint on the verandah in the extreme weather conditions that Melbourne produced in both summer and winter. I would not miss the dubious roommates I often had to tolerate who had no respect for my property or my feelings.

My mood seemed to lift almost instantly. I very rarely felt depressed these days and I had a new zest for life. The loneliness and despondency had been lifted from my shoulders. Shirley and I were a perfect fit and there was barely a cross word between us. We were both considerate of each other and had regard for each other's belongings. We were equally neat and tidy which suited us well. My old room was so cold, but the new room was warm, well maybe it was and maybe it wasn't. All the warmth probably came from just being with Shirley.

The other advantage of a shared room was a feeling of love that resulted from someone actually caring about you. If a resident was unwell and therefore had to stay in the room on a working day it was not uncommon that a staff member of the hostel would not check at all during the day to establish the condition of the resident. It was not unusual for a girl's condition to worsen which would go unnoticed for some considerable time particularly if they resided in a single room.

Shirley had shared a single room, and the verandah, with Heather when she first came to the hostel. Heather worked at the Melbourne Museum and told some enthralling stories about her workplace.

Shirley did not like her first living arrangement and therefore immediately a non-share single room became available she subsequently moved, but as our friendship became stronger we hoped that eventually the opportunity would arise to have a double shared room together.

Shirley came from Adelaide and only saw her parents approximately twice a year. I discovered she had come through difficult times. I ascertained that Shirley had an inner strength that I found phenomenal. The courage she showed was incredible. The year before she went to live at Doery House was her final year at High School. Her mother made her go to Melbourne from SA where they had lived for 4 years. She informed me that she had been happy at school although her home life was awful. Her Mum was trying her best to engineer the move back to Melbourne and she thought she could do that by moving Shirley and her siblings. Her Dad would have no option but to follow. It was all very crazy, and it only got worse as time passed. She ended up living with her aunt and going to school.

Shirley said she felt like an alien because her story was so remarkable and there was so much turmoil in the background. She felt she was a good student but in the most important year of her secondary schooling her mother had turned things upside down and that her Dad had just let it all happen.

Shirley's brother also suffered in his schooling as he was often left to his own devices and started to wag school. He suffered from this lack of parental care and supervision but tried to fit in with his friend's families.

As with myself and so many other residents, Shirley did not delight in her time at the Y but as she had acquired a good job in the city of Melbourne, there were few accommodation options for teenage girls in the 1960s. Shirley's sister Diane was a nurse at Prince Henry's Hospital in St. Kilda Road, as was my sister Anne. Diane and Anne resided in the Nurses Home at the Hospital. Another resident, Sylvia, also had a sister at Prince Henry's Hospital.

Shirley had two Auntie's living in the suburbs, one who lived at Moorabbin and the other lived at Clayton. She was also fortunate to have her Nana living in Union Street Prahran, she had resided with her for a short while when she first came to live in Melbourne. We would often catch the tram to visit her Nana who lived in a council bed-sit. Shirley liked to visit her Nana because she felt she did not have much company and was a 'loner'.

I felt a tinge of sadness when I left Shirley on Friday mornings as life at the Y on weekends could be quite dreary.

Shirley told me that she particularly liked it when I invited her home for the weekends as she missed her family in South Australia. From time to time both Shirley and Olivia would travel to Upper Beaconsfield to be with my family on weekends. Shirley went more often than Olivia as Olivia had her family in Foster to visit. Because I had to work on Saturday mornings in my father's business the girls would amuse themselves while they waited for me to finish. Shirley found my house to be very quiet without much laughter. My mother fussed over the girls making sure they had enough to eat whereas my father was stern and imposing. Shirley and Olivia felt extremely privileged and as they were the guests they were allowed to have the first bath.

There was such little water in the drought ravaged country and as each home and property survived on tank water then every drop was precious. The bath would be half filled daily then my father would always have the first bath, then my mother, then each child in order of age from oldest to youngest. Of course, if there were guests they always took precedence over everyone else. At the time this all seemed very normal as it was the arrangement used in many country households. I hated this setup, but I had no control over this system, which was long ingrained in our family, I felt particularly sorry for the last person. The colour of the water after the last person had bathed was frightful. They were probably dirtier than when they had lowered themselves in to the tub.

And why was my father allowed first bath when he was by far the grubbiest?

I thought Shirley's job was impressive as she worked for the PMG (in the public service) in the Accounts Branch in Lonsdale Street Melbourne as a clerk in accounts payable. She was a base grade clerk and that position did not involve typing – she was at a level 2 and 3 while at the Y. She travelled by train to work and earned, what seemed to me an absolutely enormous amount, $48 per fortnight, but then Shirley was also especially intelligent and knowledgeable, but not in an arrogant and egotistical way.

Olivia also had a wonderful working life at the leading accountants Peat Marwick Mitchell in Collins Street Melbourne, in the MLC building. She was a 'Girl Friday' in the accounts department completing typing and shorthand. She used a Franking Machine for the mail and also performed ledger entries. Olivia was also paid well earning $19.50 a week. I was quite envious of the girls having somewhere to go if they were running late or locked out of the hostel. Olivia had relations at Brighton and also a friend at Queen Mary Hostel that she could stay with. Like all the other residents she did not like staying at the YWCA, but she came from Foster in South Gippsland and had little choice but to stay at Doery House.

I met a lot of different and interesting people once I roomed with Shirley, as Shirley was much more outgoing and discovered information about residents that I would not have been brave enough to glean. One person that was particularly fascinating was the niece of one of the Roycroft family who were famous for their Olympic medals in horse equestrian events.

Shirley and I often had our lunch made up each day by the kitchen staff at the Y. It did cost 25 cents but was worth it as some of the milk bars charged much more. Although it was a basic white sandwich with luncheon meat or Strasburg and a little mustard or gherkin it was edible. A piece of cake and an apple or orange made for simple but filling midday sustenance. If one forgot to order lunch there was always the basket of apples on the side table in the dining room but it was not advisable to get caught placing an apple in your jacket pocket.

Some conditions at Doery House seemed very strict and others quite lax. The mail was placed on the wall to the right as one entered the building. Large quantities arrived daily as for most residents it was the only means of communication as telephone calls were extremely expensive. I wrote to my parents regularly along with my grandparents, my Nana, my great aunt and many friends. Much time was consumed with pen and paper. Thankfully my mother provided the stamps, probably procured from my father's business.

Clean sheets were provided weekly to the girls. If the dirty sheets were not presented at the laundry room then clean sheets would not be provided on the laundry day. If a resident missed out then they would have to wait another week, but to some girls who didn't care too much about this they were not fazed in one way or another how long the sheets stayed on the bed. If a resident was unwell or had an unfortunate accident it was treated as almost a criminal offence and obtaining clean sheets was not a simple process. In fact, it was so complicated some girls didn't have the energy to go through the process preferring to wait until the scheduled laundry day.

The mail, as received was placed behind lengths of elastic criss-crossed on a cork board. This mail was available to anyone who entered the foyer. None of the mail was scrutinised to check if it was actually ending up in the hands of the correct recipient. This being said very rarely did mail go missing or did girls complain about the system. On the whole the residents were a trustworthy lot. This would not appear to be the feelings of the matron though as all the girls had to request permission to leave the hostel for the weekend. They also had to sign the book situated on the lectern near the office at the front door if they were leaving for the evening.

We shared a happy room that actually got lovely winter sun but was then somewhat shaded in the summer. From the window we could see where the actor George Mallaby lived. He lived in a converted flat. He was very handsome and was starring in the Australian crime series 'Homicide'. When possible the girls would watch it on Channel 7.

We both loved music. We would sing to music on the radio. The Mamas and the Papas song 'Dream a Little Dream' got a great workout. Music and Australian Bands played a big part in the lives of teenagers in the 1960's. 'The Teen and Twenties Newspaper' was available for 15 cents and many consumed the information it contained. The most popular singers and groups were Normie Rowe, Lynne Randell, Tony Worsley, The Twilights, Jeff Phillips, Johnny Young, Ross D Wylie, Bobby and Laurie, Ray Brown and The Whispers, Johnny Farnham, Colleen Hewitt, Brian Cadd, Ronnie Burns and Russell Morris.

A lot of the girls had a portable radio in their room. Stan Rofe on 3UZ was widely listened to as he always seemed to promote the latest performers. Stan Rofe was influential for the residents at the Y in introducing them to new artists and new record releases that they would not have been exposed to if not for him. Some of the girls would use their time to find out where new bands were performing while the ticket prices were still relatively cheap. Popularity meant higher prices.

Female music devotees were shattered when Normie Rowe was caught up in the Australian conscription ballot and had to do a two-year stint in Vietnam with the Australian Army. Many girls broke down in tears as he was idolised by many and was at the peak of his singing career.

One of the great annual events in the music world was 'Hoadley's Battle of the Sounds'. Bands that had often not been seen or heard by a lot of music lovers would perform in front of a panel of judges to win the contest which included a trip to England. All the girls at the Y loved the 'Battle'.

The television provided many avenues to see the singers and bands the girls liked. 'Kommotion' was on 5 nights a week but the artists did mime their songs. 'Go Show' was on one night a week and very popular, but the artists also mimed. I would have liked to watch 'Uptight' on Saturday mornings on Channel 0, but I had to work, and the five dollars my father paid me was very important to maintaining an acceptable existence in the city.

Many of the residents of the hostel enjoyed the magazine 'Go Set' as it was the first authentic Australian rock and roll magazine. It had lots of great photographs that many of the girls would cut out and save. It had a sales record chart that was popular in enabling the girls to choose their next record purchase. There was heaps of news on everybody's favourite band and lots of information that everyone devoured. Some girls were happy to share the magazine, but a lot were not. Molly Meldrum wrote for the magazine and he seemed to have all the gossip. It was a time when the Easybeats were very popular and every week there seemed to be new snippets about them.

One of the paramount events that came out of the 'Go-Set' magazine was the 'King of Pop Awards'. The magazine was targeted at teenagers so the poll that was run was specifically aimed at capturing the young people who were the listeners of the music and the purchasers of the records. The results were shown on television on 'The Go Show'. The winner in 1967 and 1968 was Normie Rowe and then in 1969 Johnny Farnham won.

The girls at Doery House liked watching the Logies each year but couldn't understand that it appeared Graham Kennedy always won, and he seemed to be targeted more at their parent's television viewing. Every year it was hosted by Bert Newton and even though he did a pretty good job some of the girls wanted a change to someone younger. Some of the girls would buy the TV Week magazine so they could get the coupon to enable them to vote for one of the categories. None of my friends voted as they were all of the feeling that it didn't matter who you voted for the same people seemed to win. They used to think it was pre-arranged or possibly the winner had so many friends and family members that they were doing all the voting. It was significant that only Australians could receive a vote and therefore win a Logie. The coveted award was the gold Logie.

Shirley, Olivia and I often went out, sometimes catching the tram to Poppa's Pizza in Toorak Road for the most amazing pizzas in Melbourne. There was a delicious fish and chip shop in Swan Street.

One year we went to the Melbourne Show together and even bought or were given some sample bags. We managed to find plenty to do that did not cost anything and therefore had a fun day out for very little money.

Another year we went to the Moomba Festival and the parade. We had to be there early to obtain a good vantage spot.

There were ways to have fun on a budget. Window shopping was great after catching a tram to Chapel Street or making tracks in to Little Collins Street to the Coles Cafeteria Ladies Lounge where a cup of tea and a slice of pound cake or Madeira cake cost 'next to nothing'. There were always the junk shops to scavenge through in Swan Street that provided a couple of hours of entertainment. If I spent the weekend at the Y or it was a public holiday, and my friends were dirt poor like me, then we could walk to the MCG, through the Fitzroy Gardens, on to the Treasury Gardens and past the Parliament House. This way we did not have to even gather together enough money for the tram.

There were many downsides to the early closing times. One-night we girls went to the movies in the city to see 'Dr Zhivago' only to miss the ending because they had to be back at the hostel before closing time.

11

THE BLOOD BATH TO CLEANLINESS

The shots rang out so loudly that Shirley and I thought we were the actual targets.

Was that really a body on the footpath?

Completing the weekly laundry at the Y was not exactly the highlight of the week but it had at least been an outing away from the suffocating building in Church Street where they resided.

But after the latest experience would we ever venture out again to do this mundane chore away from Doery House?

The Y had an antiquated laundry of sorts at the back of the main building. There was no washing machine with a spin dryer, no stainless-steel troughs, no tiled floor and certainly no decent lighting. It was the original laundry from the days when the main building was constructed. Not a penny had been spent on it since the ancient building had been erected some time prior to 1855, and from all accounts not a penny was likely to be spent on it in the near future. There were plenty of other areas at Doery House that needed refurbishment and therefore the laundry was unlikely to see any funds come its way for many a long day.

The cold washing space with its timber walls had rattly

metal doors that did not seal properly and allowed the wind to whistle through the antediluvian scullery. There was a copper and an old single agitator washing machine that did not have a spin action. To expunge the water from the clothes one had to put them through the old mangle wringer. I had not used one of these before but rapidly learnt to keep my fingers away from the rollers unless I wished to end up with injuries to my prized bodily sewing equipment. Both my grandmothers had these old wringers in their laundries, but I had never had the misfortune to facilitate myself of them. The double laundry troughs were made of concrete and Matron told the girls there was a time when a double concrete laundry sink was a sign of affluence.

Was this supposed to make the girls feel privileged? For if this was the case it certainly was not having the desired effect on the residents.

There was also a scrub board at one end of the trough which had seen better days.

There were no plugs which had been misplaced or stolen long ago. I bought my own plug but that too disappeared after I inadvertently left it in the laundry one evening. It was replaced by my mother with a stern warning that this was not to be a regular occurrence; consequently, this second plug was closely guarded. There was a small supply of dolly pegs and these were certainly needed for the clothes line which was not the hills hoist type that I had been used to but was a single long line of heavy wire, strung between a tree and a

135

post at the side of the laundry. One needed to use the handmade timber prop, or all the clothes would end up dragging on the ground. It had a V notched in one end to slip under the line and a pointed end to anchor into the ground. I recollect that my Nana also used this method to dry her clothes. I also recalled that it was fraught with danger because the timber prop may become dislodged, particularly in times of high wind, and then the whole lot would end up on the ground. It was not a time to be around Nana when this happened. This was also true at Doery House as many of the girls got a great giggle from the sight of the Bombay bloomers hanging on the line that obviously belonged to some of the well-endowed staff at the Y. Woe betide anyone who allowed this oversized underwear to fall on the ground when negotiating the clothes line. This was particularly not a good idea if the said items were wet and they ended up with grass, leaves and dirt stuck to them. Many a girl ran away, with a sprint worthy of the Olympic Games, when this happened. I once saw this unforgivable occurrence happen to a girl I had never met. She left them on the ground as she refused to touch them or rinse off the particles that were stuck to the undergarments. It caused great hilarity amongst the girls.

The whole laundry experience was so time consuming and demoralising that I was pleased to discover that the reason I rarely saw other residents in the laundry was the fact that they bundled up their laundry once a week and walked down Church Street,

136

turned right in to Swan Street and spent a pleasant hour chatting and gossiping with girlfriends while their washing went round and round before their eyes.

The other great benefit was that their clothes were washed and dried all in the one outing without having to put the clothes on the rusty old line at the Y. There was another valid reason that I used the Laundromat as in the summer of 1967/1968 there was a thrip plague in Melbourne.

One afternoon when I arrived home exhausted from my day at work, along with the long public transport trip home, and ending with the task of walking up the steep Church Street hill in the blistering heat, I ventured out the back door past the television room to collect my washing from the line. It was a 39 degree day so I knew my washing would be well and truly dry but I got more than what I bargained for when I discovered my white underwear covered in tiny black insects that had managed to invade and stick to every part of my underclothing. It was impossible to remove them from under the elastic in my undies, in fact I burst in to tears when I realised they were all ruined and that I would have to dispose of all the items. No matter how much I picked and brushed the undies, and rinsed and rinsed the items, the horrible little critters would not leave all the tiny crevices they had invaded on my underclothes. I once again went to my mother with a sad tale of woe and again my mother came to the rescue.

After all what could she do?

I was ever so grateful that my white uniforms had not

been on the line as the cost of those was another matter that my mother would have been most displeased about. This convinced me that never again would I use the laundry facilities, such as they were, at the YWCA.

I had already been warned about the perils of using the Laundromat - the risk of cross contamination, health problems, thrush and much more. After all, all manner of bacteria could grow in that steamy environment and who knows who had used the machine before me but with all the warnings I was willing to take the chance as I wasn't going through the prospect of another thrip invasion on my clothing.

The pleasant hour with my friends all changed one evening as Shirley and I were watching the large washing machine agitators whirling around and around before our eyes. As this mindless action happened we chatted about work and some of the amusing things that had occurred during the day when the unfolding events happened in a flash of horror. All of a sudden shots rang out.

Shots, a body on the ground, people yelling, men running, guns, sirens and police.

Was this a normal evening in Swan Street?

Lying in bed that night Shirley and I wondered if it had all actually happened.

We crouched down, we looked out the window of the Laundromat, the washing machines continued to whir, and what could we see, blood running in to the gutter. Following the shots, we heard the heavy footsteps of people running. The footsteps were getting louder and louder as they approached us. It seemed of little use to squat down in the Laundromat, but we didn't know what else to do.

As we clung to each other for support we saw four men running past the window, at speeds that would challenge a competitor in the Stawell Gift. One was ahead of the other three and was obviously being chased by three very rough looking men who were yelling a barrage of swear words interrupted regularly by the word 'stop'. They looked frightening with their tattoos, unshaven faces and tight leather jackets. To finish of the alarming picture, they all had their fingers wrapped around sawn-off shotguns. They had no regard for the body on the ground, they didn't even check to see if their victim was alive or dead, they simply jumped over the guy on the footpath as they were more concerned about the pursuit of their next quarry.

Did anyone care about the dude laying on the concrete where every crevice and crack of that concrete was slowly filling with blood?

Wasn't anyone going to check if he was alive?

As we heard more shots ring out we decided it wasn't for us to decide the outcome of the blood-spattered fellow on the footpath. Other people walked past but no one seemed to do anything with any urgency and there was no way Shirley and I were venturing out of that Laundromat.

All the girls at the Y knew about the gangland issues,

the mafia and the Painters and Dockers, the union that covered the docking of ships amongst other things. It was talked about from time to time, not by the matron or staff at the Doery House but by the residents themselves. They knew there were some shady characters around Richmond, some of them being violent and dangerous. It was a well-known fact that there were some major crimes in Richmond, along with the small-time criminals, vandalism and juvenile delinquency. All of these showed no sign of abatement, as was the case in many working-class areas in Australia.

Parts of these conversations did not shock me as my father owned a trucking business and they carted many loads of supplies to the docks for transportation. I had heard my father's conversations with his employees about the wharfies. Even though my father acknowledged that the wharfies worked hard, it was a tough job even with an improvement in the 1960s of modern cargo and container handling, he also spoke of their standover tactics. They seemed to control the workforce which included the hiring, firing, rosters and payment extras such as overtime and work allowances. These caused all sorts of problems for the transport companies as strikes or restrictions occurred at the wharves. Any trouble from employers or officials including the police or customs could see a full-blown strike or wharfies walking off the job. It was something my father lamented but knew it was all part of the industry and he had to cop it even when it caused great disruption to his business, especially when he was carting fruit from Northern Victoria's fruit district. The wharfies knew that they had the power and could often hold up important shipments that had a big impact on the country. Any crimes on the docks that the police tried to investigate meant a strike was imminent. Many of the wharfies were union tough guys with the Painters and Dockers. The Federated Ship Painters and Dockers Union represented labourers in the shipbuilding industry. There were many gangs with leaders who were the toughest of the tough.

The girls at the Y had heard about the standover men, the prostitution, the drugs, the gambling and the gangland battles, but they had not seen anything firsthand until now.

Finally, lots of sirens were heard and even though the police and ambulance had arrived we did not know whether to leave or stay. Emergency people were frantically trying to save the guy on the ground as he was being loaded in to the back of the ambulance.

Wasn't anyone going to clean up all that blood?

The police eventually came in to the Laundromat and asked us endless questions for which we knew very little and much of this questioning went unanswered, after all we were in shock. The constabulary were extremely persistent in their quest for information, but we could offer little help, as we were both traumatised, not that they realised this at the time.

When Shirley and I arrived back at the hostel, with our clean clothes neatly folded in bags, we ran in to the television room yelling, 'Guess what? Guess what? We just saw a crook shot in Swan Street outside the Laundromat?'

The other girls wanted to know all the grisly details and they were so wide eyed that we added a few bits and pieces to the story. We had to be careful not to embellish the story too much as police had our addresses and informed us they would want to re-interview us. Sure, enough four days later they presented themselves at the Y. And didn't the matron love these dramas while she was in charge. Even the thought of a police car at the gate or a police officer knocking on the door gave her heart a flutter.

Who knows what happened if they knocked on the door or wanted to make contact with matron or one of the girls outside the ridiculously restrictive opening hours?

Matron sat in on the interview and wanted to know every gory detail. She kept going over and over the happenings with endless persistence. She was worse than the police. She seemed to want to lay some of the blame on us for actually being there at the time of the incident, and informed the two of us that no good could come of venturing in to Swan Street after dark.

Didn't we know that there are unsavoury people wandering the city streets at night? Despite the best efforts of the police in insisting that Matron did not interrupt she continued to do so and when they finally left they did not appear to be satisfied with the results of the questioning.

Shirley and I considered abandoning our weekly laundry visits to Swan Street but despite the curse of the strain on the budget we couldn't bear to use the hostel laundry facilities unless we were desperate, and we were not that desperate, all I had to do was think back over that ghastly thrip plague. I remembered vividly how rinsing my underclothes over and over had made little difference as the little critters had even got in to the weave of the fabric. They apparently had a passion for white clothing of which I had my fair share. Much of the underwear was so badly infested that it had to be relegated to the bin. To save a little extra money I would have to take the dreaded train on Sunday night from Flinders Street to East Richmond and walk up Church Street rather than catch a taxi. This would save $4.50 which would make a big difference, meaning I could also afford the money for the Laundromat washing and drying machines. Obviously I wasn't thinking clearly when I made this decision because at any time I could have had an encounter with one of the many disreputable people that were lurking around the streets of Richmond.

The trips to the Laundromat had to stay, shooting or no shooting.

I wondered at times if I should take some sort of martial arts lessons to protect me from the perils of Richmond after dark but where would I get the resources for that?

The night held a constant reminder for us in the form of the footpath stain. Nobody appeared to clean the mess up immediately after the shooting. No amount of foot traffic and rain over the coming months seemed to wash away the last remnants of a life that may have ended.

12

CHOCOLATE COATED THIEF

Each and every day, hail rain or shine, I was summoned to the reception area to receive the lunch order for the La Petite owner, Mrs Rogers. At first I didn't like this duty, but then I found it was a way to get out of the workroom and out in the thriving metropolis of Collins Street and see what Melbourne people were doing and wearing.

Sometimes Mr. Rogers would also require lunch, but he usually stuck to his tried and true simple requirement of a ham and salad roll. On very rare occasions he would have a curried egg and lettuce sandwich, with strict instructions to make sure the sandwich bar worker applied a decent layer of butter but no salt and pepper. By looking at him one could see where the butter went.

Mrs Rogers changed her order every day without fail; it seemed to depend on her mood what her requirements were. One constant was the need for wholemeal bread. No white bread for her. Wholemeal was starting to become trendy as the usual white bread was being rejected by those who thought wholemeal was healthier.

I would head down Collins Street to the sandwich bar. The staff making the sandwiches and rolls worked behind a display cabinet full of salad items and a variety of meats. There were also packs of readymade items for those who didn't have time to wait for a custom-made sandwich or roll to be made. Mrs Rogers would have none of the pre-packaged items as she didn't consider them to be fresh. Along the side of the entry to the sandwich bar would be racks of wrapped cakes, chocolate bars and various sweets. Standing in that queue made my mouth water. The array of things that were for sale was totally out of reach for me. The lunch I brought to work each day that I had pre-ordered at Doery House had to suffice each day.

I often saw Carol in the queue. Carol commenced at La Petite around the same time as I did but she worked in the tailoring section. I did not know who she purchased lunch for, whether it was for another staff member or just for herself, but we often said hello to each other and passed a few words as the queue progressed. I did think it was a little odd that Carol was often overdressed for the weather, frequently wearing a heavy coat in the middle of a heat wave during the summer.

I was more interested in the fashions, including shoes and handbags, than noticing what was happening with those in the queue. That was until one particular day I noticed Carol slipping something in to her pocket.

Was I mistaken, was the item going to be paid for when she reached the counter? This did not happen, but I thought maybe Carol had inadvertently forgotten to pay for it. Each day as I waited to order Mrs. Rogers latest lunchtime craving I tried to act nonchalant about life and focus on the other happenings in Collins Street, but my peripheral vision was able to capture the daily thefts that took place at the hand of Carol.

One day as Carol came out of the tailoring section, which always seemed so much quieter than the finishing area, she virtually knocked the side of my leg as she was descending the stairs from the finishing room. I remarked, 'You are going to get caught one day.' Carol looked slightly taken aback but replied, 'I don't know what you are talking about.'

I decided I had to do my utmost to avoid Carol in the lunch time queue; this was not easy as all the La Petite workers had the same lunch time allocated each day.

Unfortunately, or maybe fortunately Carol was eventually caught but much to my horror she named me as her co-conspirator, and she informed the police that I was used as the decoy in the queue along with her theft exploits. The police found it difficult to pin anything on me as apart from Carol's statement there was no evidence. My work locker and personal items were searched. Our work colleagues were also interviewed proclaiming they had never seen me with chocolate bars or packaged cake at work.

It came to light during the investigation that Carol always purchased and paid for something at lunch time, but the items placed in the pocket of her coat, that she always wore, far outweighed those that were actually placed on the counter with the necessary coins. At first it seemed the shop owner was oblivious to this shop lifting but after some weeks Mr Pocock started paying more attention to the customers in the queue. This all began when he noticed the rack at the shop entry needed re-stocking far more frequently than it had previously. He discussed the matter with his staff who verified the stock was disappearing quicker than it was actually being presented at the counter and paid for. It turned out that Polly Waffles were one of Carol's favourite treats, a clever shoplifter would have alternated or rotated their desires, as it soon became apparent to the shop owner that the Polly Waffles were disappearing faster from the stand than those that were actually presented at the counter for payment.

While I was cleared of any wrongdoing and being falsely proclaimed as being named as part of Carol's mischief, the shadow hung over me all of my days at La Petite. Mrs Rogers chose another young employee to complete the lunch time task of standing in the queue at the sandwich bar. Subsequently this did not help my feelings as I felt 'a bit of the mud had stuck' and I was guilty by association even though I hadn't done anything wrong.

Approximately a fortnight went by when one evening the police turned up at Doery House wanting to re-interview me. They informed me they just wanted to clarify some of the matters relating to the charges against Carol.

Matron commented later to me 'that trouble seemed

to be following me around, first the Laundromat issue, now this'. I didn't need this pointed out to me and was upset at Matron's snide remarks as I wasn't exactly happy about these dramas arising in my life either. Life sure wasn't dull and boring outside the four walls of the YWCA. Matron actually seemed to enjoy all these events in the life of Doery House as it gave her a chance to exert her power and authority.

Now that I didn't have the arduous lunch duty for the Rogers each day I found myself with a little time to explore other parts of Melbourne.

I enjoyed going to Degraves Street which ran between Flinders Street and Flinders Lane as I could explore the wonders of The Little Bookroom which was devoted to children's books. It took me back to my childhood that was filled with wonderful reading memories. When my mother visited the city, she would always return to the country with a Noddy Book or one of the latest Girls Own books for her daughters. These books were much anticipated and were read and re-read many times and then swapped between the girls and read again. I loved to read and thankfully there was always an abundance of books in my life. My love of reading never faded and it was often a saviour in passing away the boredom and constraints of the YWCA.

I also liked to gaze in the windows of the many establishments in Flinders Lane as it was the epicentre of the rag trade that I was so closely associated with.

I loved Melbourne's arcades and gazing in to the

many windows as window shopping did not cost a cent. My favourite haunts were Block Arcade, Royal Arcade and Centreway Arcade. On rare occasions I would indulge in some chocolates from Haighs in Block Arcade, but I could only dream of taking high tea at the Hopetoun Tea Rooms.

All the diamonds and gold were worth dreaming about in the window of the clockmaker Thomas Gaunt & Co in Royal Arcade. At the end of the arcade was an enormous clock that chimed every hour. That clock was a reminder to me that I must return to work on time or face the consequences.

There was so much history in the Melbourne lanes and arcades, marble, cast iron in the domed ceilings, columns, mosaic or terrazzo on the floors, faded paint, worn steps in to the shops, lots of stone and the smell of times gone by to fill every sense that I had. It seemed to me that now I lived in the city I just could not get enough of it.

That was well and good on a clear day but if one had to venture across the Princes Bridge along Swanston Street on a wet and windy day then you would have to hang on to your scarf and hat or it would be blown into the Yarra River. Putting up an umbrella was perilous as it would inevitably be turned inside out or worse still ripped from your hand and sent flying into the river to float away never to be seen again.

I found the bargain basement at Myer fascinating. It had a myriad of items that were marked below their original asking price, although most of them were still out of reach for me on my meagre wage.

As I browsed amongst the collection of tables displaying all manner of items, it crossed my mind on more than one occasion, the ease with which someone like Carol could have carried out her shop lifting in the bargain basement.

While walking down Collins Street approximately two months later much to my horror a voice said over my shoulder, 'Would you like to do a spot of shop lifting?' As I turned around, I did not at first recognise it was Carol sporting a new short bob haircut and wearing glasses.

Our paths never crossed again much to my relief.

13

THE GRASS IS NOT ALWAYS GREENER

Sadly, for me the dream of working for a high fashion house in the city of Melbourne did not last long. I found the hours, the pay and the ruthlessness of the rag trade difficult to endure. The pay was so poor my parents had to give me almost the equivalent of my pay again, each week, just so I could exist. Most of my pay was taken up by the weekly board at the YWCA and for that the living conditions were poor.

I was extremely frugal and only spent money on the bare necessities. Some weeks it was difficult to make ends meet. As a junior I had been treated poorly at La Petite although I did enjoy my work colleagues and some of the creations I was involved with. I knew that I would miss the finishing work and the high-class beading creations I was involved with.

I saw an advertisement in the daily newspaper for a junior at the fashion house called Magg, situated in Toorak and owned by the Holts, of Prime Minister Harold Holt fame. The wages were higher, and I would not have to go into the city to work. My parents were dismayed at this change but decided it was best to allow me to make my own choice about my workplace, and after all I was still in an industry where my talents would be utilised, or so they thought.

From the minute I arrived at Magg I realised I had made a big mistake. I was treated even more poorly than I had been at La Petite and I was given the most menial jobs. I was not able to do any beading or finishing work as I had done previously, all my creativity was suppressed. Even my co-workers treated me as someone that you gave the basic and tedious work to because it was beneath them to do the job themselves. I quickly hated that trip to work each day. Here I was in accommodation I disliked and a job I detested.

Eventually I just up and left Magg without knowing what I would do next or with a firm plan for the future. All my friends at the hostel were sympathetic and offered to help me find a job but I insisted that I must find my own career path. Ringing my parents with this news was not pleasant.

When I walked out of Magg I went straight to the nearest phone box to inform my mother that I was now unemployed. My mother was aghast and verbally expressed her dismay as to what the future now held for me. Full of bravado I told her that she was not to worry, that I would find another job, although I didn't tell my mother that I had no idea what I would do. One particular thing I did inform my mother about was that I was firm in my thoughts about definitely not going back into the rag trade. This was to add further to my mother's consternation as that had been the whole purpose of relocating to the city after receiving a glowing reference from my class teacher.

I scanned the papers for the next week looking for a new position and it did not take long for a new career path to present itself. I saw an advertisement in the positions vacant in The Sun News for a junior dental nurse. Experience was not required; training would be completed in the dental practice and three years' study at night school was required to become fully qualified. I wondered whether to tell my parents before an interview or after. After much contemplation I decided to go for an interview and wait for the success or otherwise of that meeting before talking to my parents. If I told them prior to the interview I was fairly sure my parents would put the kybosh most decisively on this new vocation path, especially as there was more travel involving two modes of transport to and from work.

I went for my interview in the full knowledge that I knew nothing about the dental industry but from the minute I arrived, in my nervous state, I realised this was right for me, and all the way home I prayed that I was successful in obtaining the position. I did not have to wait very long as the call came within twenty-four hours informing me that I was indeed successful and could I commence the following week.

Now indeed it was time for the difficult element in imparting the news to my mother and father that I was indeed going to be a dental nurse in the suburb of Port Melbourne which was certainly nowhere near the hostel at Richmond. To say they were shocked would be putting it mildly and they even tried to discourage the idea, but I was adamant that this was what I wanted.

It was obviously third time lucky as I stayed in the wonderful working position for seven years, I loved it with a passion. I thrived on the long working hours and the study.

I had abandoned the rag trade, but I knew that even though I had chosen the lengthy trip to my new chosen career it was the correct decision. From the first day at work I never regretted my choice to follow another career path in my young life.

Early each morning I left Doery House for the walk down Church Street to the East Richmond station. This was done whether it was oppressive summer heat, or the gale force winds with driving rain on winter days. I travelled to Flinders Street where I walked to platform four to catch the train to Graham Street Station at Port Melbourne. The alternative would have been to catch a bus from the city but although the fares were cheaper it would have made the trip longer. When the train arrived at Port Melbourne I had a lengthy walk down Graham Street to Bay Street where the dental surgery was situated on the corner of Bay Street and Graham Street, Number 136 Bay Street.

When I was employed at La Petite I thought that my feet were always painful but that had been trifle compared to what I had to suffer when I accepted the position at the dental surgery. I was required to wear flat brown shoes and there were plenty of these available, but I wanted something that did not appear to have been made especially for the Matron at the YWCA at Richmond. As always my resources were limited so I had to choose wisely. Sadly, this did not happen. I should have chosen something unremarkable and less fashionable as I was on my feet 95% of the day and those trendy brown shoes with the small heel may have looked good but they were not made for comfort.

I quickly realised that times had changed. Back when I was a small child and even further back to my parent's childhood, teeth were filled over and over again. Most teeth were eventually extracted if they were decayed and were causing toothache. The large majority of elderly people had dentures, it was an important event to have all one's teeth removed in the 1930s and 1940s and even in to the 1950s as a gift to celebrate one's twenty-first birthday. Both my parents had dentures.

Most people travelled into Melbourne proper as that is where most of the dentists practiced. It was a long arduous trip for country folk. I began to realise over time that this must have been quite traumatic for a lot of people and not really a gift to rejoice in.

During these days the West Gate Bridge was being constructed. Construction commenced in 1968 (This bridge was to collapse on 15 October 1970, two days after my birthday, 35 people were killed.) This was not a pleasant time for me as twice daily I had to walk past the mammoth construction site. I was young, fairly attractive and had a good figure. Despite being dressed in a nurse's uniform I was an easy target for the many construction workers, young and old that I passed along the way. A considerable number of workers could see me long before I rounded the path from the railway station. From their vantage points high above the ground they were able to wolf whistle at me, some with an extremely loud pitch which alerted their co-workers and ensured that the workers on the ground were ready with their lewd comments. Some girls at the YWCA considered a wolf whistle a sign of admiration but I found it to be nothing more than a frightening form of sexual harassment.

Each day as I approached Graham Street Station to begin the walk down Graham Street to the surgery I felt the panic in every fibre of my body. Some days were worse than others but never was there a lack of anxiety in my stomach and my ever-increasing heart rate was always evident. On occasions my heart pounded so hard and fast I thought my chest would explode. If I managed to make it to the footpath along the road before I received any unwanted attention I could relax just a little, although never completely, as on some rare occasions there were workers near the construction site huts where the engineers, architects and supervisors congregated. One could hear the whirring noise of the air-conditioners in these demountable prefabricated buildings the closer one approached as they must have been like saunas in the summer and like cold storage facilities in the winter.

My return journey in the afternoon was never as harrowing as the morning. Most of the workers started extremely early in the morning and were gone before my trip back up Graham Street.

On my twice daily trips down Graham Street there was one older more mature guy who didn't seem to share in the antics of his work colleagues. He watched on with an eagle eye but never participated. He was tall, with a neatly trimmed beard. He had curly dark hair and a muscular body with arms that looked like he was a body builder, neither slim nor fat. He certainly was imposing but somehow he was not frightening, although he had an air of authority to him. I had to admit my level of anxiety was not as great when this guardian angel was in view.

One day in early 1969 I was travelling up Graham Street feeling fatigued after a particularly harrowing day that had been packed with new patients all requiring large quantities of paperwork. The surgery work was also challenging with lots of cases demanding more work than was scheduled. Thrown in to the mix of the chaotic day were several emergencies. I had to admit later I was in a bit of a dream, the sun was going down, and I was not paying full attention to my surroundings when the unexpected happened. From the back of one of the construction huts appeared a large burly guy with a pot belly stomach, tattoos covering his arms and a cigarette hanging out the corner of his mouth.

Since arriving in Richmond and many surrounding areas, including Port Melbourne, I found that many people smoked cigarettes. I found this very different to my way of life as none of my family, my relatives, friends or neighbours smoked. Very few of the girls at the YWCA smoked and certainly none of the girls I had become friendly with. It was considered to be the domain of the working class. Wherever I went, particularly when I was travelling on the train I saw billboards and neon signs spruiking the necessity and the advantages of buying Marlboro or Craven A. The sight of all this advertising was almost enough to set off an asthma attack for me.

Late on this evening walk to the train the perceived danger or threat was telling me to flee, hide or freeze, but what to do?

I was paralysed as the burly guy suggested that I go with him to the hut as all the other workers had left for the day.

'You really want it, I have been watching you for days, flaunting yourself and teasing all the other guys.'

I did not respond as I was in so much shock I was left speechless as the burly guy walked towards me in an extremely imposing and threatening way.

'You think that you are so high and mighty in your nurse's uniform believing that you are untouchable.'

Still nothing, why couldn't I speak?

He was now only a short distance from me, and I could feel the cigarette smoke getting into my lungs.

I was so frightened that panic threatened to overtake me completely as the burly guy grabbed my arm with such force I cried out in pain. Despite being rooted to the ground I was dragged forcibly to the hut. I now knew it was too late for flight, so I had to fight, but the terror in me was so immense that I felt powerless to defend myself. My attacker tried to rip my two bags from my arms, but I held on tight feeling they gave me some kind of protection.

'Have it your way, keep your bags, but it won't be so easy to keep your clothes'.

I did not know I could scream so loudly and with such a high pitch but as the perpetrator tried to rip my uniform from me, and the buttons down the front started to give way I let out a sound that surely most of the residents of Graham Street must have heard. It was time to put up an almighty fight as I tried to hit my attacker with my bags, I was kicking and scratching. The only problem with this is that it made my attacker exceptionally angry and more determined to have his way. I felt I would rather die than let this person rape me. Sadness overwhelmed me when I realised this may be the end of my life.

'Get off her, I said get off, you scum, leave her alone'.

Who was that pulling the burly guy from on top of me? I finally focused to see that my guardian angel had come to my rescue.

'So, you want her first, that's okay I can wait until you are finished, just make it quick, I need to get home' said my attacker.

Next thing I heard a loud wack and then another worse one, then I saw a lump of wood swinging through the air hitting the burly guy in his chest. As I sat up it looked like my attacker was out cold on the hut floor.

I was shaking uncontrollably.

'Are you okay?'

My guardian angel called for a taxi to take me home.

He paid the driver and he assured me he would look after his work colleague and that this perpetrator would never trouble me again.

I got home okay and took the next day off work. Thankfully I did not have any serious visible signs of the attack apart from a large bruise on my arm which was not noticeable when I wore my cardigan. Thankfully my uniform had not been ripped but several buttons needed to be sewn back on to the front opening.

It was unknown what happened on that Westgate Bridge site from that day on, but I was rarely targeted even to the sound of a wolf whistle. Sadly, though I never trusted the people on that work site and was careful to finish work before dark every day.

And what happened to my guardian angel, I never saw him again, I hoped he had not been punished for the attack on the burly guy, and for saving my life?

14

DEAR DOCTOR

Next to the YWCA, as one headed towards Bridge Road, there was a stately old home where a doctor had his medical practice. The house had previously belonged to the current doctor's father Dr David Roseby and his wife.

He had a never-ending supply of patients from the Y as there was always someone with a female problem or two. One wondered if it had always been a medical practice or if it was just fortuitous that Doery House was right next door with a never-ending source of girls that required assistance of the healing or therapeutic nature.

Dr Roseby was a kindly, gentle, understanding Jewish man who treated all the girls from the Y like his own daughters. To visit Dr Roseby, one had to go through a small gate on the right-hand side of the house. This gate was attached to a brick pillar that proudly held the brass plaque that displayed Dr Roseby's name and his qualifications. The plaque was highly polished and well maintained as a symbol of the upstanding doctor within the practice. In the spring there were always colourful bulbs flowering in the garden. They always lifted one's spirits and gave a cheerful welcome even to those unwell souls coming through the gate. I wondered if it was Dr Roseby or his wife who kept the garden so beautiful, or maybe they had a gardener. As my grandmother was an avid gardener I recognised the Japanese maple, the jacaranda, the magnolias and the crepe myrtle. There was even a tree dahlia covered in pink blooms.

The small waiting room at the front of the house had polished timber floors, some uncomfortable dining room type chairs and a matching low table which held some old magazines. Though these magazines were old they were no match for the prehistoric magazines that were placed in the front sitting room at Doery House. The chairs were veritably modern compared to the ones for use by visiting guests at the YWCA.

Dr Roseby was a portly man, had spectacles, always greeted his patients with a smile and very rarely kept them waiting. All the other girls at the Y could have taken their female problems to matron but this was not worth considering. She was a spinster and would have promptly dismissed anyone who came to her.

Many girls had monthly problems, but Dr Roseby would not allow this to go on month after relentless month before he promptly issued a prescription for the contraceptive pill to alleviate further problems. He was a very modern and practical man. He also prescribed the pill for girls who requested it as he did not wish to see any of his charges coming to him with a distressing tale of being in the family way. He knew that their life in the city and their chosen career would come to an abrupt end if they became pregnant, not to mention the fact that they would be given their marching orders from the Y. He certainly was a forward thinking, caring, no-nonsense doctor whom the girls could approach without fear on just about any subject.

For those who went to Dr Roseby with the terrible thrush condition, he believed the laundromat in Swan Street was the problem, but he also was a practical man who believed the facilities at the Y were sub-standard. He knew the girls visited the Swan Street premises because they felt they had little alternative. He also believed they did this with trepidation as they all feared a repeat of the sighting of the recent shooting. Hence he would hand out the required prescription and his interminable invaluable advice on how to eliminate or reduce the risk of re-infection. I used his recommendations and advice during my whole life and passed on Dr Roseby's message to many others.

I made frequent trips to the doctor. A visit cost between $2.00 and $4.00 but on some occasions he would waiver the cost as he knew most of the girls earned very little money, especially the juniors, trainees and apprentices. Almost all the residents fell in to this category as the Y was already charging them a premium for accommodation.

Dr Roseby had a young family and he and his wife regularly went out to dinner at some of Melbourne's finest restaurants, along with socialising with many of the other professionals in the city at many of the premium events frequently held. His picture could be seen in the paper from time to time at some spectacular event in the city. This meant he needed a babysitter from time to time. When he asked me if I was available to babysit for him and his wife, I was delighted, and subsequently when he informed me what the payment would be I was over the moon with excitement.

Why hadn't this happened when I needed to buy the necessities of life?

First things first though. A time was set up to meet Mrs Roseby to pass the obvious test of suitability.

What if Mrs Roseby found I was not suitable and was lacking the standards required to assist, and therefore possibly not up to the task of looking after their young children?

When the time came to see Mrs Roseby for once my shyness did not overtake me and I found the words to speak eloquently and succinctly about why I would be the right person for them to hire.

During the discussion I also found out that Dr Roseby had been, some years previously, the President of the Victorian Branch of the British Medical Association. I also discovered he was a champion of the 'new Australian' or refugee. He believed that if Australia had not given his family refuge many years ago he would not be a hard-working Australian doctor. He was interested in my work as a dental nurse in Port Melbourne and the array of nationalities that frequented the practice every day. He was pleased to hear that one of the dentists I worked with was Italian and that he spoke fluently to his Italian patients. Many Greeks came to have work completed and so the Greek nurse used her skills to converse with them. We also saw lots of Yugoslavs and Lebanese each week. The dental practice built up quite a reputation for its multiculturalism and was always extremely busy. The fees were very moderate and hence anyone who had a toothache would appear on the door, some were even waiting before the door opened each day.

Dr. Roseby was the son of a poor Russian Jew and therefore he was fascinated to hear that my great grandparents were called Solomon and Rosetta. He believed there must be some Jewish background in my family if they had those names. In the late 1960s the 'White Australia' policy was abandoned and consequently more migrants arrived in Australia. I did not see any change in my workplace as it was commonplace to have a mix of cultures as regulars at my place of work. Racism seemed to be commonplace but not where I was employed. Australian born residents seemed to mistrust and dislike 'new Australians', and that included British migrants, until they proved themselves.

I told the Rosebys that when I was only fifteen years old my mother had taken ill after the birth of my baby brother, Andrew. Her lung condition was part of the problem and consequently she was in hospital for a considerable amount of time. My older sister Anne had also gone to hospital as she had contracted rheumatic fever. Father worked long hours and had a business to run. My younger sister, Ellen was only thirteen years old and the baby, Gaye was only five years old, so I had to run the household for the rest of the family. This included the washing, cooking and cleaning, and it was all while I went to high school, travelling 3 hours a day on public transport to and from school. All the washing came home from the hospital that belonged to my mother and older sister. In amongst all this I had to get my homework completed and continue studying.

I informed Mrs Roseby that when my mother returned from hospital, she was so grateful that she gave me a book called Cookery The Australian Way and on the inside cover she wrote 'To Rosalie, for being so helpful to all the family during my hospital stay, with fond love, from mum'. All this information that was imparted obviously impressed Mrs Roseby, who must have thought I was mature beyond my years and would be able to manage any challenge that may occur and therefore they promptly gave me the babysitting job. I didn't realise when I arrived at their home on that cold blustery winter day to be scrutinised that any concerns I may have had quickly disappeared as Mrs Roseby was just as kindly as her husband, speaking to in a caring, gentle, almost sing-song voice. And I also thought she was so beautiful.

We agreed on a time for the first job. I explained that I could only babysit on weeknights unless I was given several weeks' notice as this would mean I would not be able to go home for the weekend. I was informed that I would be paid double for Friday and Saturday night, much to my delight. I gave the Rosebys a list of the lock up times for the YWCA and the strict rules about complying with the closing times. Secretly I hoped that they would not ask me to babysit too often on the weekends or if they did they only made requests for Friday nights as I really did not want to forego my trips home at the weekend. They were very important to my wellbeing and the weekends at Doery House made me melancholy and so lonely, almost depressed.

When I arrived at the Rosebys 'mansion' the following Wednesday night I discovered just how big the house really was. I had never imagined that there was a large expanse of rooms contained behind the Doctor's surgery and waiting room. Upon my arrival I was taken upstairs where I found it difficult not to stare at the magnificent drapes at the windows, the thick luxurious carpet, the superb furnishings, the artwork on the walls and the ornaments that adorned the sideboard, the mantel piece, and the various other pieces of furniture. I tried desperately to concentrate on the instructions that Mrs Roseby gave me. I was given advice on the TV use and was also furnished with a contact number for the Rosebys while they were away from the house. When I was taken in to the kitchen to be given my instructions on making a hot drink to go with the supper that was laid out on a plate, I thought I had gone to kitchen heaven. I loved to cook, and this room looked like a dream where every recipe could come to life with a minimum of ease.

And the supper before my eyes, was it really all mine? It certainly was nothing like the Y crackers and

Madeira cake that they were served most nights with the weak Ovaltine.

The two older children attended the very best public schools and were in Year 1 and Year 3. They were still awake when I arrived, but the baby aged almost 2 was in bed already. I farewelled the Rosebys with an air of confidence although underneath I felt anything but self-assured. The butterflies in my stomach soon disappeared as I had no trouble connecting with the two children as we all got on immediately. I even found it relatively easy to put them to bed after an endless amount of games and book reading, some they read to me and some I read to them.

It was a very windy night in Richmond, up on top of the hill in Church Street. It seemed like every wall was rumbling and creaking, every tree branch was rubbing on the outside of the house, and every window rattled as the gusty, swirling wind continued to pummel the old house. At times I thought the roof might actually lift off the house completely. I found the house on this first occasion to be spooky, apart from several quick checks on the children I stayed stuck to the couch until the Rosebys arrived home.

Strangely I grew to love that house and all its occupants. With each visit it became less and less eerie, and I soon looked forward to my times there with the added bonus that it took me away from the boredom and loneliness of the Y. I always took some hand sewing with me which I enjoyed, away from the noise of the Y utility room near the telephone area

When I finally left the YWCA at the end 1969, after three years of living at Doery House, I thanked the Rosebys for having such a wonderful impact on my life and told them I would miss them more than words could describe.

Sadly, I never saw them again.

15

BOYS, BOYS, BOYS

When the United States navy boats came in to port, usually at the Williamstown Naval Dockyard there was great excitement at the Y. I listened to the chatter and laughter in early 1969 when the one such naval boat arrived in Melbourne at the Dockyard. The word quickly spread that the sailors and crew from the ship were up for a good time which meant plenty of dancing, food and beverages, and of course the inevitable extras at the end of the evening were expected by many.

Countless girls wanted to participate in the outings and despite pleas from several of the residents at the Y, I always declined to join in. I was labelled a prude and a stuffed shirt for this, but I was not concerned by these comments one little bit. Why would I give up my virginity for some drunken sweaty seaman from another country that would never be seen or heard of again?

It was the beginning of drug taking as a social activity and hence there was plenty of marijuana and LSD around. There were also unknown prescription drugs in plentiful supply. Usually the seamen didn't partake for fear of the consequences in their working life, the penalties for them if they arrived back at their ship intoxicated were feared by all, but many drinks were spiked to make the girls more relaxed and accommodating.

In the autumn of 1969, I heard numerous girls getting ready for their big night out, giggling with excitement. Most of them had miniskirts on that barely covered their swaying backsides, and there were the inevitable hotpants which allowed the cheeks of their bums to show out of the lowest parts of the pants as they teetered on their high heels. The shift dress was also very popular as long as it was above the knee and sleeveless. Many of the girls used or wasted their late pass, whichever way you looked at it, for these parties which I thought were a sheer waste of a somewhat valuable resource that was not easily obtained.

Girls were often locked out on these nights. In the late 1960s the closing times at the Y were very strictly enforced and those that were in charge at the Y were not concerned if the young girls slept on the street or worse still, that they came to grief at the hands of some ghastly perpetrator. Rules were rules in relation to closing times and every resident had to abide by the closing times, without exception. I often pondered on this arrangement which frightened me as Richmond was not exactly the safest place to allow someone to wander the streets at night. The large gate at the front of the Y lead along a concrete path to the front door. Either side of the gate was a large white block wall about six feet in height. Often girls would come in the gate late and with nowhere to go they would sleep on the grass at the front of the Y shielded by the high fence. This was all well and good in the summer but for protection in the winter the only place was the tiled front verandah which was not a comfortable place to spend a few minutes let alone a whole night. And it was not worth thinking about what Matron would do if she found you there in the morning when she unlocked the large wooden front door. The offender would be chastised in no uncertain terms.

Often the girls realised too late that they wouldn't make it back in time for closing because they were often affected by alcohol, drugs or just the fact that they were having a plain old good time. Consequently, at the time they were not anxious or have a feeling of foreboding as that came later when they returned to Doery House.

One such person was Jean. She met her sailor friend, Chuck in the city. This was normal as the girls were very rarely collected at Doery House by the seamen. They went on to Flinders Street to the Trocadero where there was always a dance happening. In fact, any girl who wanted to drop in to the Trocadero looking for a good time could always do so, particularly if a ship was in dock and the place was swarming with sailors. They always looked very slick without a hair out of place; obviously the use of Brylcreem was a saviour.

The first night out for Jean and Chuck was so enjoyable that they arranged to meet again. Jean was amazed that Chuck took her back to the hostel in a taxi and she was home in time for the Friday night closing time of twelve midnight. A lot of the sailors gave girls money for the tram and sometimes on the infrequent occasion they were put in a taxi to go home but they were rarely personally escorted to the front door.

Jean thought Chuck had been a thorough gentleman and tremendous company, he hadn't even tried to molest her or made suggestive comments let alone tried to have sex with her. She bragged to all the other girls and it seemed to everyone that she had hit the jackpot with Chuck. She said he danced like Fred Astaire or Gene Kelly and knew all the right moves. She told everyone that she wasn't very light on her feet but by the end of the evening Chuck had made her feel like Ginger Rogers. He had even bought her a lovely necklace that he said was set with two genuine emeralds. Gifts were sometimes given to the girls by the sailors but nothing of this quality and worth.

Jean had applied for a late pass on the Saturday night and she could barely wait for the taxi to arrive at Doery House at 6.00pm. She had decided to wear the short shift dress that I had made her in black and white stripped fabric. She didn't wear stockings as this was no longer the trend since the English model Jean Shrimpton attended the Melbourne Cup in 1965 without stockings. Jean Shrimpton had helped women to assert the right to proudly parade their bodies as they wished. Shorter skirts had become an image of the general culture of a revolution that characterised teenagers and young women in the late 1960's. Jean wore a stunning pair of black and white high heels. One of the many hairdressers at the hostel had swept her hair up in to a beehive style and her makeup was done by one of the other girls who was completing a beautician's course. Jean was ready long before the agreed time of retreating with her newly acquainted beau.

At 6.00pm sharp the handsome leading seaman, Chuck, arrived at the door of the Y. He wouldn't hear of Jean waiting on the footpath. All the girls swooned as they caught a glimpse of Chuck. Many made excuses to pass by the front door or quickly ascend the stairs to the verandah to ogle at Jean's date.

That night Jean did not arrive back at Doery House in time to use her late pass. It appears not only was Chuck a good dancer, but he was also a noteworthy actor. The passing of the previous twenty-four hours proved that all was not as it had seemed one day ago. The evening started well as they headed to the St Kilda Town Hall for a dance. Chuck suggested they head in to the city for a drink and to listen to some music while they got to know each other better. Jean says she remembered the last song clearly was the Righteous Brothers song 'Unchained Melody' thumping in her head. As Jean became more and more tipsy and obviously intoxicated she later described a feeling of not being inside her own body, a sensation that she was looking from the outside at herself or even a different being. This was all happening while Chuck was putting into motion his well-planned systematic arrangement. As it was late he suggested that they get a room at the Southern Cross

Hotel. Wow, thought Jean, the hotel is upmarket and has an exceptional reputation.

Why not?

Chuck had been such a courteous, noble man and has such great taste she believed. When they arrived at the hotel Jean sat in the foyer, luxuriating on a leather lounge with plumped cushions behind her back, all the while trying to focus her blurry eyes and head on her surroundings. Her handsome partner was making the reservation at the check-in counter. Jean looked up a few minutes later to see a well-rehearsed forlorn looking face. 'Sorry honey, they are fully booked, but don't despair I have a contingency plan', he said, as he pulled her to her feet from her position on the lounge and headed towards the revolving glass entry doors. Jean spoke later of a feeling of almost been lifted off the ground or not being in charge of her own movements. It was obvious by now that Jean was so lightheaded she wasn't aware of where she was going or where the name of the destination was.

Jean vividly remembers the pain that followed. Chuck had obviously planned his sexual intercourse with her or was it just plain rape?

How many times in her befuddled state she would never know, but the high level of pain and the amount of bruising suggested it was many and brutal. He did have the good sense to put her in a taxi but by the time she arrived back at the hostel the sun was coming up on Sunday morning. She sat on the front entry until the front doors opened at 7.00am. Even if she had rung the bell or knocked on the door earlier it would have been fruitless as no one would have opened the door anyway. When Matron saw her there she did not display a glimpse of compassion as she viewed the dishevelled Jean. She wore only one shoe and her dress was a crumpled mess with the zip stuck half way down as it was caught in the fabric at the back, her hair was in disarray and there were streaks of mascara down her face. Matron virtually dragged her in the door and told her to gather herself together in her room. There was no sympathy and no questions about whether she was alright or needing any assistance.

Most of the girls at the Y were taking the contraceptive pill, thanks to the foresight of Dr. Roseby. Birth control was introduced in Australia in the 1960s. It had a substantial bearing on society, allowing girls and women sexual independence. It did stimulate lots of argument about promiscuity and sex before marriage. Many mothers were against the notion of their daughters requiring birth control, but teenagers in the 1960s, including those at the Y, did not want to be limited to the perceived roles that the world had apportioned to them. They wanted the freedom to have sexual intercourse when and where they wanted it and did not necessarily want to wait until marriage. Jean was one of a number of girls who was taking the pill. She was grateful for that fact after the encounter with Chuck, especially as two months later a letter arrived with a USA postal mark. Jeans hands were shaking as she read the contents that revealed Chuck did not use a condom when he forced himself sexually upon her. The letter did not actually divulge this fact, but it was apparent when she read the contents of the letter. The arrival of the letter indicated that Chuck had some sort of morals it seemed or maybe he was remorseful as when he returned to the USA he was diagnosed with a sexually transmitted disease. He subsequently made the decision to inform Jean and possibly all the other girls he had seduced in every port around the world.

The cries of 'no, no, no' rang through Doery House. Floods of tears appeared and there was no consoling Jean. It was Friday evening when the letter arrived, and Jean was the first person on Dr Roseby's doorstep the next morning. Dr Roseby's endless words of wisdom were the panacea for this catastrophe. Jean mulled over his words indicating that things may possibly have been worse if she had not been on the pill and the night had ended with an unwanted pregnancy.

The following week Jean decided to go the pawn shop to get rid of the emerald necklace that Chuck had given her. Much to her dismay she found out that it was worthless, and the so-called emeralds were actually glass. As she left the Easy Money pawn shop she threw the necklace in to the nearest rubbish bin realising it had only been given to her to loosen her honour and make her more susceptible to agreement when it came to sexual favours.

The next ship that sailed in to the docks with many a desperate, sexually starved sailor on board saw very few Y girls take up the offer of a night out on the town.

16

UNCOVERING RICHMOND

I found Richmond a dingy, jam-packed, chaotic place at first. There were strange terrace houses made out of weird coatings that looked like plaster or material that was used to make headstones in a graveyard. I was to learn later from Lia, that this was called stucco, very Italian, very woggy. As it turned out those wogs and dagoes and reffoes and ethnics, as they were called, were not only of Italian descent but also Greek.

The Italians lived in Richmond well before the Greeks arrived, so no wonder there was an Italian influence in the buildings. I met local resident Lia one day as she was leaning over the gate that was the entrance to her neat little front garden. Lia was able to chat, with ease, to her neighbours and the people that passed by at almost any time of the day. She was always extracting bits of information about the area. It didn't appear she was gossiping or being a busybody, but she did love a chinwag and enjoyed gleaning secrets and revelations from all manner of people.

At first I tried to cross to the other side of Church Street to avoid Lia but after a few pleasant exchanges I was happy to chat to her. It was a way of finding out a bit more about this new hometown I was now a part of.

I knew I had an ally if ever help was required when travelling up and down the street. I was worried that Lia would delay me if I was rushing to catch the train, but it soon became evident when there was no time for a chat.

Some of the houses in Richmond were also quite grand and seemed like mansions, despite the fact that some were also pretty spooky. One such house was Lalor House which seemed absolutely enormous to a country girl. It was on the same side as the Y but heading towards Bridge Road. It looked almost ghostly at night when there was only one light on in the upstairs section. It was also a doctor's surgery, but all the girls preferred to visit Dr Roseby's. These grand houses had tiled or slate roofs with mosaic tiled verandahs whereas the terrace houses mostly had corrugated iron on their roofs and painted concrete verandahs.

The houses for the working classes were also made of timber and most were single fronted. There was the odd brick veneer house amongst the timber houses, a lot of them having striped awning blinds to keep the sun out and to protect what little furniture they had from the harsh summer heat. A lot of these houses were quite small, but they often had to house reasonably large families. Many had large concrete pots or containers on their concrete terrazzo tiled verandahs. It seemed a strange sight that many residents had gone to the trouble to put plants into their small front gardens but did not take the trouble to water them. These newly planted shrubs or flowers, be they in the garden or the ugly pots, were often left to wither and die, never to be removed. It was almost as if the owners were relaying to all passersby that they had made an initial effort and that was enough.

In other areas of Richmond, such as North Richmond and West Richmond, the Housing Commission was building flats. Some people were not happy with these high-rise monstrosities, but others were pleased to move into a brand new home, especially the people who were the first residents. These were usually those who had had their homes resumed and demolished to build the flats. The ones who were displeased were those who had been paid a lesser amount for their home than the true value. There was also a stigma attached to those who lived in public housing. Lia said she was glad she couldn't see them from her house in Church Street.

Some of the faded notices in the windows of a number of the establishments in Church Street intimated that they would take boarders. By the state of the sign it was unknown whether they had ever been successful in their attempt to find a lodger, or they had many vacant rooms, or the room had been filled and the owner had been too sluggish to remove the sign from the window. Nevertheless, the worn, pale signs did not entice a newcomer to knock on the door to enquire about becoming a resident. If the sign was any indication of the rest of the premises maybe it was better not to venture inside. Although it could also suggest that the rent may be cheap and affordable.

I always felt that Richmond had a strange aroma to it as if the whole suburb needed a good wash. It was a suburb full of new Australian workers who had brought with them many and varied smells particularly in their food preferences and cooking habits which seemed to waft up and down Church Street.

Class humiliation was rife in Richmond and as such the suburb was part of a working – class reserve. Alcohol and a lack of work were two of the big problems. The area had poverty and community issues that required social workers supplied by the council.

On one of my many trips down Church Street I learnt that Lia had not long ago installed a hot water system in the house, along with the addition of a washing machine. Like the Y, the laundry was still an archaic affair at the end of the path from the back door. The convenience of an indoor laundry was probably never going to eventuate as the tiny home barely had space for the occupants as it was. She also told me that some years ago; they had placed some much-needed carpet in their living room. They purchased it from the Piano and Furniture Warehouse, Maples in Swan Street. There were strict rules about that carpet though. The family had to be shoeless to walk on it and had to have spotless feet. There was most definitely no food or beverages allowed in that room. She was very proud of her hot water system, her washing machine and her carpet. Lia also said that some of their friends had bought furniture on hire purchase from Waltons. They had done this many years ago and were still paying for it now after the furniture or electrical appliance had long worn out or gone in to a state of disrepair.

There was another trap for those who were easily conned by door to door salesmen who knocked on the door at mealtime endeavouring to sell encyclopaedias. They often cost over a thousand dollars and would take years to make the payments. The information contained within the books was long out of date, but those payments still had to be met. Those who didn't pay up would be taken to court. The fine print in the contract was very difficult for many new Australians to comprehend. Lia said she had never fallen under the spell of salesmen either at the door or in a shop. She believed if you didn't have the money to make the purchase then you needed to wait until you did. It was all a matter of budgeting.

Lia told me of a school that her nieces, Angelina and Flavia had attended in Richmond that had been built to such a low standard that the walls and roof were at risk of collapsing. Plaster would also fall off the walls regularly and the building was only 10 years old. I was aghast at this news as I had not been exposed to such matters in my short life.

Some of the building standards and regulations were extremely poor in the first half of the 1900s in the lower-class suburbs but thankfully they were improving Lia believed. She was quick to tell me that the new Richmond High School was excellent, and it was the school that her two youngest children were happily attending. Apparently the built up working class suburbs had been suffering from a lack of good quality schools for many years. Richmond Girls School, she informed me, was not the place to go if you wanted a real education as they taught mainly Commercial subjects and home economics. She also told me to be careful of any of the Richmond Tech boys as they had a reputation for being pretty rough. Lia herself sometimes had trouble with her English but she had been forced to speak the language when she arrived in her new homeland. And even though the words that had previously been used to describe her and her fellow countrymen had been replaced with 'New Australian' she felt that the use of dagoes and wogs were terms of endearment and not meant to offend.

The words New Australian sounded like these new arrivals had to be segregated from the people who had been born in Australia. Lia said she and her family had become naturalized as she was very proud of her new country and wanted others to feel the same.

When Lia arrived in Australia she felt joyous when she disembarked at Station Pier at Port Melbourne to begin her new life, the streamers that were being thrown from the Pier linking the boat made her feel connected with a great sense of being welcomed in to her new country. She immediately knew she would be happy in her new homeland.

Lia said they were making progress on many fronts as they had even rebuilt the Richmond Railway Station, although it was still quicker to walk to the East Richmond station or catch a tram. Apparently the old

Richmond station must have been in a terrible state as it had been condemned.

Lia was happy with her lot in life and did not hanker for a more ostentatious life. She was happy to catch the tram to St. Kilda beach on a warm sunny day with her husband and children. They were even able to venture to the Dandenong Hills on occasion with her husband's family as they had two cars. She even proudly told me she had been to the Globe Theatre and the Richmond Theatre on two occasions and had seen Dr Zhivago, which made her cry, and The Sound of Music which had made her very happy. She considered her life was fortunate although I felt there was a touch of sadness that many of the Italians had moved out of Richmond to be replaced by the Greeks. Lia told me that there was a lot of unspoken discrimination which may have been the reason for the changes.

Many Greeks and Turks had moved into the area and some places were overflowing with occupants, many more than the building could cope with. I had to admit I felt a little intimidated by the Greek men who would sit in the upper level of some of the buildings in Church Street drinking and gambling of an evening. They would call out comments to me in their native tongue which obviously were lewd, and it was probably best that the girls at Doery House did not know what had sprung forth from their mouths. They played very loud music that sounded like something from the movie, Zorba the Greek, and they could often be seen dancing with their arms waving in the air. While the men were playing cards, their children were running around downstairs, shouting and screaming, often way after what was considered bedtime.

Some stores had begun employing multilingual shop assistants to encourage New Australians into their stores. Even the Health Centres needed interpreters for all the mothers with their new babies that were populating the area. I saw many young mums pushing prams up the steep incline of Church Street. Some of the signage or notices were being placed in churches and buildings in English, Italian and Greek.

The census in the 1960s indicated that there were over forty percent of New Australians living in Richmond. Some of the old-time residents were not happy that the new inhabitants would not speak English but preferred to speak in their mother tongue thereby upsetting the people who only spoke Australian English. It was sometimes felt that these newcomers were speaking ill of the Australians who could not understand what the conversation was about. It was one of the many challenges for all as some New Australians had very little knowledge about how to converse in their newfound country. There was some disunion amongst different cultures as people found it difficult to mix when the requirement was for enormous amounts of tolerance. Often the older members of the families who had migrated to Australia did not speak English and hence this added to the cultural breakdown.

Lia was extremely economical with the use of her

resources as were most people during the 1960s, and she prayed at St. Ignatius church up on the hill that she and her husband could survive on her meagre savings and the pension. She told me on one occasion that I looked pale and anaemic, and that I needed to eat more fruit and vegetables. 'You should visit Magnanos,' she said. I did not have a clue who or what Magnanos was. A few weeks later a small package of fruit was pressed into my arms as I lumbered up Church Street in the heat. This turned out to be a regular occurrence, but it was many months later before I was to discover that Magnano's was a fruit shop that was a family run, much loved business with superior merchandise that operated opposite the Globe Theatre. I did not actually get to visit this revered fruit shop as Lia kept me well stocked in all manner of delights of the fruit variety, some I had never seen let alone eaten before.

I also learnt about Kanis's café that was on Bridge Road, along with Missy Lou's milk bar that was on the corner of Bridge Road and Punt Road. It was run by a very nice Chinese family. The best time was to go on Saturday afternoon as once the footy had started it was very quiet. All the games were played on Saturday after lunch but once they were over it was teeming with people in all the inner suburbs.

I was warned to be careful after 5.00pm on a Saturday after the football as many people either drank too much in celebration of a win or drank even more when their team lost.

It was important to stay away from Squizzy Taylor's

billiard room which was above Cecil Johnson's Barber Shop. Lia laughed and told me that everyone got the same hair cut whether they wanted it or not. Most were fashioned around a pudding bowl cut and if one had a fringe it was always cut too short, whereupon one was the laughingstock of all they met until the hair grew out. People continued to frequent the place though as it was the cheapest haircut in Richmond.

I received with enthusiasm the history of the St Ignatius Church that had been constructed using contributions from the large number of Irish Catholics that had originally been in residence. The church had been designed by William Wardell and built between 1867 and 1892. The foundation stone was laid in 1867 so it was a slow process to construct the church. It did open in 1870 but it was a long road to completion. This same Irish Catholic population made Richmond a Labor Party stronghold. Lia told me that she had a couple of friends who were not Catholic, they attended St Stephen's Church and as this was a Church of England Church Lia's husband was not pleased with the relationship.

Many of the older generation did not like to mix with religions of a different persuasion. This theory was firmly entrenched in many people as history would show that back in the mid-1800s when The Roman Catholic Church wanted to buy a property for St Ignatius Roman Catholic Church in Richmond the owner of the said land would not sell because he was a man of the Church of England faith.

Lia attended St. Ignatius on Sundays, along with a lot of her friends, family and neighbours. I was told that if one missed a mass on a Sunday then there was always another one as they were held on a regular basis from midnight on Saturday and then all through Sunday. Each service of mass was packed, even the confessionals were packed as all Catholics went to the confessional box at least once a week. Lia said it was not only the spiritual aspect that was important to her but also the social and emotional advantages she received from her connection with the church. As a Catholic, Friday night was always fish and chip night which the whole family looked forward to. When I told Lia about all the wogs from Greece that came in to my workplace she told me I could go over to Holy Trinity Church in Burnley for some Greek lessons.

Lia had a cousin, who seemed extremely old to me, his name was Guido, and he had a wealth of knowledge and history in his Italian brain. He chatted easily and this is where I learnt so much about the past life in Richmond along with the many changes. At first I was a little irritated by Guido's constant chatter, but he was so engaging and humorous I soon became caught up in his infectious love of life and the stories of times gone by. I had to admit I even looked forward to it and at times as I walked up Church Street if Guido was nowhere in sight I was somewhat disappointed.

As I was so interested in Balls and Dimmeys, two of the places I frequented on a regular basis, I was voiced in the background of these establishments by the exuberant Guido. I was enthralled with his knowledge and discovered that Dimmeys was the home of the gold-rush drapery Dimelow & Gaylard. It was large and successful, a business admired by many. In the very early 1900s it was purchased by John Sims Jeffery after the previous owners had been operating it for about 25 years. They were refused the use of the existing name so "Dimmeys" was born. After all this was already the nickname used by local shoppers so why not make it the permanent title. Guido gushed that even country people could buy from Dimmeys using their mail order department of the business. They even manufactured on the premises, producing ladies underwear, millinery and manchester products. Guido laughed when he informed Lia and me that they even had bra fitters to attend to all the ladies requirements. He thought it was a huge joke that they sold trainer bras for young girls seeking their first bra, and even had the latest fashion in the 'cross your heart' bra. I was extremely embarrassed by this talk as I had never heard men discussing the subject of ladies underwear before.

Sadly, a fire extensively damaged Dimmeys in 1907 but to the delight of the locals and customers far and wide it was rebuilt, and they even added a balled clock tower. Some said this was at the time of rebuilding others believed it was around the time of the First World War. Long before the fire Dimmeys always had a monthly 'fire sale'. Bargain hunters loved it and the store sold everything one could imagine. The building had round arches and more semi-circular arches on the windows. The clock tower had glass panels that were illuminated at night creating a local landmark that was visible for miles.

Guido told me that there was a posh, more upmarket store than Dimmeys at one stage. It was Alexander's Clothing Store. It started out as The Commercial House Drapery and was situated on the south west side of the Bridge Road and Church Street intersection, having been built by William Bust Burnley in 1858. It later became the headquarters of the Alexander's Clothing Store in the 1960s.

I asked Guido if he could tell me about the Bedggood Shoe Factory that was in a street off Church Street. Some of the girls at the YWCA worked at Bedggood but I couldn't think of anything worse than working in a shoe factory. Guido didn't know much, except that they made a lot of school shoes at the factory and it was known to be a tough place to work, with employees having to complete a certain number of tasks in a day. The wages were considered poor in comparison to some of the other factories in the area. In their defence though they were one of the first companies to mechanise production.

The local shirt manufacturer, Pelaco was also in Richmond in Goodwood Street. All businessmen aspired to own more than one Pelaco shirt. Guido informed us that if you owned more than two shirts then you were a fine upstanding businessman, well in his opinion anyway. He felt it was obvious that a Scottish man had started the business as he believed they were always so well dressed. Pelaco was also a favoured place to work as they reduced the work hours in the early 1900s and eliminated the need to work on Saturdays. Highly favourable for many was the morning and afternoon tea serving with the daily breaks. The tea was supplied by the company which was virtually unheard of by other businesses. They even had an industrial relations officer. Despite the business having many pro-active work practices most seamstresses lasted less than twelve months in the position. It was extremely difficult to find and hold girls who could stand the speed and the monotony of the minutely subdivided system of work. The introduction of piece rates had made deferential incentives to workers exceeding the set practices which had previously been put in place. The building had an enormous neon sign on top of it. Guido purported that the letters were fourteen feet in height and were in pink neon lights, therefore no one could forget the name.

The Rosella jam making factory also provided a substantial amount of employment for residents of Richmond and surrounding areas. If you had experience 'on the fruit' then you were assured of a job, it also helped if you knew someone who worked at the factory. In the past employees were paid by the hundred tins of fruit filled but Guido wasn't sure if that was still the case. It was considered a big promotion if you got to work on the lemon butter machine. Rosella also had great jobs for men especially if you had experience or qualifications in metal trades. Highly sought after was the position of truck drivers. The factory was enormous, manufacturing not only canned fruits but their famous tomato sauce, jams and chutneys. One of the things it was most renowned for was the wonderful parrot symbol that featured on all its products. It was so recognisable that customers sighted that on their products and associated it with the brand without even looking for the Rosella name. The parrot meant Rosella and resonated with the shoppers and just by seeing that wonderful bird they knew in their minds that they had a good quality product.

Guido enthused though that the business that everyone really wanted to be employed at was Bryant & May in Church Street. You 'were made' if you worked at this forward-thinking business that treated their workers like human beings. The building had been designed in an Art Nouveau style by Melbourne architect William Pitt and was constructed very early in the 1900s for the Empire Match Works. Bryant & May purchased it soon after and added another storey along with a clock tower. The company was considered a model employer and far ahead of its time, providing many benefits for its employees, including health services, sporting facilities and meals. 'Can you believe it,' Guido exclaimed, 'that they even have basketball courts available for use and a bowling green and tennis courts along one side of the building?' I was so envious as my place of employment was virtually slave labour compared to what Guido described. Wouldn't it be wonderful I thought, to have a kitchen and dining room where one worked? Bryant & May even sounded one hundred percent better than the accommodation at the Y. No wonder employees would never leave the place, giving other prospective workers little chance of securing a position there. And of course, there was virtually no possibility of securing anything remotely similar.

One of the places that Guido wasn't so satisfied with was the Richmond Power Station, also known as the Melbourne Electric Supply Company Limited. It had been used for power generation since the late1800s. New chimney stacks were erected in the early 1900s and for many, many years it spewed its smoke and pollution into the air. It seemed to contaminate the place and cause smog if the winds were unfavourable.

No wonder Richmond was a hive of activity with lots of workers cottages as there was so much industry in the area with plenty of jobs for those that wanted to work hard. Most of it was tough work but there were also some businesses that had favourable work conditions in sought after positions that offered incentives, rewards and some relief in the day for their workers in the form of meals, sport, hobbies and activities.

I learnt that some good husbands handed over their whole pay packet to their wives so that she could run the family home and pay the bills, whilst others kept some for themselves to spend at the pub, on cards or the horses. I imagined this caused a lot of friction and tension in the marriage and hoped that this would not eventuate when I actually found the right boyfriend that I would spend the rest of my life with. I wondered what happened in my own family home as there was no pay packet seeing as my father owned his own business and I couldn't imagine how the whole process worked. I did know one thing and that was that there never, ever seemed to be any money to spare. Every dollar was looked on as a precious commodity to be channelled back in to the trucking business and its expansion.

One item that I did not discuss with Lia and Guido, due to the now heavy heart I had, was the Skipping Girl vinegar neon sign that was a welcome sight for me on many a dark night when I was heading home. The skipping girl was called 'Little Audrey' and she was 25 foot high. Little Audrey was an animated neon sign, the first of its kind in Australia, consisting of a flat painted silhouette background with neon highlighting that was supported by a steel sub-structure. Whelan the Wrecker tore her down in September 1968. It was a sad time for a lot of Richmond and Abbotsford residents along with Melbournians in general as she appeared over the passing of time to be good for nothing but scrap metal after standing tall and proud for 33 years. There was a public outcry at her removal and a lot of people like me were saddened at her demise.

Lia became a much-liked resident and a welcome respite from the trudge home up the Church Street hill. She informed me that she also wanted to stay well and not to become mentally dependant on others. To me this did not seem a dream that was out of reach and a very meagre dream at that.

Lia proudly told me one day that her name meant 'beautiful rose' and that is why her husband had planted the roses in their miniscule front garden amongst the tomatoes, artichokes, beans, garlic and herbs. I did not know if Lia had ever had a job or a career but as it was the 1960s most girls got married, had children and then stayed home to look after the brood she had given birth to and the man who had made it possible.

Home duties was considered an honourable way to live your life if you were a female, although many married women with children did work as the management of the daily expenditure could possibly determine the family's destiny. Credit was not extended to families in any form and the margin for error was minute. Most shops did not extend the hand of assistance and there was no leeway if one was unable to pay for goods required. If bad fortune or hard luck fell on a work colleague many workers would do the 'whip around' to assist. This was remarkable when most families did not have even a dollar to spare each week. Banks would only lend money for housing purchases and the conditions were stringent. Despite all this Lia was one of the most contented people you could meet, despite the lack of materialistic possessions and the hardship she had endured she was still full of love, exuberance and optimism.

17

OVERCOMING BOREDOM

The girls at the Y had many idle hours to while away. There was more to life than watching the temperamental old black and white television in the sparsely decorated, antiquated television room. Spending endless hours in one's room was not an agreeable option either. They were hot in summer and perilously cold in the winter. There were no power points for heating or extra lighting and the one low wattage globe that hung from the ceiling barely gave enough illumination to the room let alone giving off enough light for reading.

Playing cards was frowned upon by the matron and the residents were frequently informed it was the precursor to gambling and would not be tolerated in the hostel, but despite the poor light it didn't stop the girls from playing card games in their rooms. This frequently happened on the sly and was supposed to be light-hearted and fun. This had always been the case until new resident Lesley arrived.

When Lesley arrived in the YWCA dining room one gloomy winter's night, in 1969, she surely looked like she could punch above her weight, as my father used to say about a person who looked strong, forceful and confident. She had all three of these in bucket loads. I was only five foot two inches tall so to me everyone looked closer to the ceiling than me, but Lesley was closer to the bare bulbs in the rooms than anyone else. As she walked into the dining room you could hear the thud of her heavy brown lace up shoes on the floor which made most of the girls look up from their vegetable soup, which I was not partaking of as it had oodles of barley floating on the surface and stuck to the side of the bowl. It was all I could do to keep the bread in my stomach. The need to retch was so great at the sight of all that disgusting barley.

A voice boomed out, 'Anyone sitting here?' as Lesley sunk on to the vinyl padded chair at the big timber dining tables. Wendy was sitting opposite me and exclaimed in a low voice, 'What have we got here? This could be trouble.'

For the next couple of weeks, it looked like everyone thought it was best to avoid Lesley. Some had discovered in the television room two nights earlier that Lesley was an orderly in a psychiatric establishment. Well that was what she referred to it as, so we girls weren't sure if it was a hospital, home or hostel, and of course as we were all scared of her no one dared ask Lesley the real identity of her employment. She had already made it known that the other residents should mind their own business unless they were looking for a tongue lashing. This was another of my father's favourite sayings and the description of same was used by him many a time within my family.

It appeared that Lesley was going to be the boss when it came to the choice of TV programs each night. She had the uncanny knack of arriving first each night in the television room, taking the prime position and setting herself up in the most comfortable chair. This was a loose term for the padded chair that had the most functioning springs in it, the least tears in the vinyl and had timber arm rests that were actually smooth. Most of the other chairs had little to no springs in the seats. Some of the other chairs also had arm rests but they had torn vinyl on the rests which scratched one's arms, so in reality the chairs without the arm rests were a better option. If you wanted to stay long term in the soulless television room then comfort should not come in to the equation. It was not much better in daylight hours as it was a very cold and dark space; therefore, it was frequented by the residents as little as possible.

On colder days Lesley always managed to pull her chair of choice as close to the electric oil heater as was possible. This heater was not renowned for emitting much warmth at all, but it was still a favoured item in the winter even if its power was all in the mind. Girls liked to sit on the heater, which was quite okay as this was a true testament to the low amount of heat coming from it, as no one was ever in fear of actually having their legs or derriere burnt. It was strictly forbidden to drape clothes over the heater or to try to dry items that were required for work the next day, but alas this did not stop some girls particularly those who needed panty hose urgently. Panty hose were an expensive item and some girls only had two pairs to carry them right through winter. They were often darned and patched until there were more repairs than was acceptable in the working world.

As Lesley was always first to the television and because all and sundry were too frightened to challenge her, then whatever she chose to watch meant all the other girls had to comply. There didn't appear to be anyone who was brave enough to confront her with a different selection. It depended which night of the week it was, but she seemed to choose medical programs or programs where she could laugh at others' misfortune. Lesley particularly enjoyed Marcus Welby MD, maybe it was the medical background she had that appealed. And then on other occasions she would roll around in fits of laughter at programs like 'I Love Lucy' and 'The Beverley Hillbillies'. 'Gomer Pyle' was also popular and she seemed to delight in taking off his accent any time of the day and night. It wore thin with a lot of the girls. Trying to outvote Lesley in her choices was also fruitless. One-night June got up from her chair, walked abruptly to the television and was about to change channels when Lesley boomed, 'Don't you dare.'

On one occasion Lesley was actually late to the TV room, when she walked in she declared in a questioning voice, 'Does anyone play cards? 'Well if you do, I'm in.' You could have heard a pin drop, nobody spoke, everybody was mulling over in their heads this proposition.

When next I got together with Olivia, Susan and Wendy for our regular card game we discussed the proposition of Lesley joining us. Wendy believed she was trouble and verbalised her feelings in no uncertain terms.

Susan exclaimed 'If we let her in, how will we get her out?'

Olivia offered, 'What if she wants to bet with money, then she cheats, and we all end up owing her a lot of cash that we just don't have?'

This discussion went on for weeks as no one seemed to be able or willing to give alternatives that everyone may agree on.

When Lesley was happily settled in to her favoured chair and watching her preferred television program she never mentioned the cards but when she was late and the weight of numbers in the room meant she would have to comply with what the majority had decided, she brought up the topic of the card games once again.

'Surely some of you play cards?'

Finally, after many weeks Lesley announced she was setting up a card match every Tuesday night in her room. She had a single room so she could do as she pleased.

I wasn't sure who joined in during the first few weeks, but sure enough Lesley only played for money. It started to ripple through the corridors and common rooms that Lesley was cheating as she rarely lost and there were some suspicions about how it was happening. If Lesley had hoped that the setting up of these matches would endear her to the other girls she was sadly mistaken as it had the opposite effect.

She was, not unsurprisingly, turning out to be a bully and many of the girls steered clear of her domineering ways. We became used to the heavy footsteps on the timber floors and knew when Lesley was in the vicinity. The one place she could not lord over the girls was in the phone recesses. You could not stand between a Y resident and the guy she loved.

Olivia went in to the sewing room one evening to let me know that Lesley had tried to jump the queue on Kathy as Kathy had been about to ring her boyfriend in Echuca. Kathy had been waiting somewhat patiently until her turn eventually arrived for the phone. There was an extremely heated argument when Lesley arrived proclaiming she had an urgent call to make.

'Bad luck,' said Kathy, 'join the queue.'

A loud argument broke out but the other girls supported Kathy and eventually Lesley went to the back of the queue with her hands in fists she proclaimed to all and sundry in a disgruntled and threatening voice, 'I won't forget this.'

I was part of a Euchre card club back in my hometown. I had been taught by the best and had been brought through the ranks using tough tactics by the instructors. I was told I wouldn't learn anything if they went soft on me or let me believe winning was easy. I was taught how to count cards, how to store information succinctly and very importantly how to spot a cheat. It was important to me that when I went home on weekends I still managed to get to the Euchre club regularly.

All of this had been swirling around in my brain since I had become aware of Lesley's card games and the possibility she was cheating. I did some homework and established that no one had divulged the existence of the illicit card games the girls had been a part of for months if not years, so Lesley was probably under the impression that she had the only set-up.

But how was she cheating?

They usually played 500 which was similar to Euchre. Could I somehow get in on the set-up and request they play Euchre?

I knew from the gossip around Doery House that the loss of money to some residents was getting out of hand so I decided to have a chat to the girls who played with Lesley, to see if they knew how to play Euchre and if not would they be willing to allow me to teach them. And so, began Euchre lessons on the side. Once the girls became competent I informed them they now had to see if Lesley played Euchre and if they could switch the game of choice every now and then. This was all taking weeks and weeks of planning and still some girls were losing a considerable amount of money.

Finally, a lucky break came. Brave Ellie told Lesley she wouldn't play anymore 500. She was bored with it and wanted to play Euchre. This was Carol's opportunity to inform Lesley that she would be away for four weeks on holiday but I had wanted to join the group so I would be taking her place.

I had done a lot of work and planning with my fellow card players and felt they were ready. I was confident that if they could remember their cards and count correctly then Lesley would be done for. I was also one of the few people that knew about the rat. I knew in my mind that it was a sick pun, but I felt like that may be the trump card.

Once I joined the group things happened quickly. I knew that Lesley was reneging in some rounds and that more than one pack was being used. Next round, I thought, the game was progressing, and I pounced, 'you reneged.' Lesley had kept back a playable card in one round as it would have disadvantaged her if she had laid the card. The girls backed me and sure enough when looking back through each 'trick' that Lesley had supposedly won she had reneged at least once. Lesley was of course all apologetic and innocent in appearance. A few smooth rounds followed and then the same procedure again.

'You are a cheat Lesley. How much money have you won with your cheating ways?' said Shirley.

It wasn't so easy for the girls to see your indiscretions when playing 500 so it was pretty straightforward for you to pilfer more money from these unsuspecting girls. 'Hand back all the money you have stolen from them including some for Ellie,' I said.

'No,' said Lesley, 'You can't prove it.'

My reply came fast, 'I just did and if you don't do as I

say I will go to Matron and let her know you set up these games and coerced us all in to joining you with your bullying and your threats.'

'Also, I will inform Matron about your pet rat,' I said in an abrupt voice.

The look on Lesley's face was one of resolution and defeat. She knew she had been beaten at her own game.

'You wouldn't would you?' exclaimed Lesley.

'I will and I know quite a few girls who will help me get rid of it permanently if we have to,' I replied.

The strange thing was that nobody had physically seen that rat. Some of the girls had talked about their thoughts on Lesley having a pet rat.

Shirley told me she didn't think it was possible.

'No way,' said Shirley, 'you aren't allowed to have pets at the Y.'

'Anyway, how do you know?' Lesley questioned.

I told Shirley that one night at cards one of the girls had sworn she had seen a giant mouse scurry from under the bed to the other side of the room and then disappear under the wardrobe in Lesley's room. Wendy thought it was a rat there and then. When she screamed at the sight of the rodent Lesley told her she was imagining things and that she should keep quiet or Matron would come and investigate and then their card games would definitely be shut down. According to Olivia she had seen Lesley dropping food in her coat pocket at dinner one night. I absolutely hated rats and mice, as did many of the girls, even though they were a common sight in the homes in the country. It would be much better if that horrible rat saw a permanent end, but I wasn't completely heartless and so that was definitely one final thing I couldn't impose on Lesley, no matter the dubious character of the girl.

I didn't know where I got the courage, but I stood over Lesley while she went to her dresser drawer where she kept her ill-gotten gains. As she opened the drawer for all to see there were over 20 packs of cards.

'And what have we got here?' I laughed, as she showed the other girls.

The cards tumbled from her hands as she scooped them up partly with glee and partly with discomfort at what had been happening for months and would have continued if I hadn't implemented a plan to trap Lesley. Lesley looked frightened for the first time since we had all known her and genuinely looked afraid that the girls would set upon her. She then forthwith took a chain from around her neck that held a small well-worn silver key. With this key she opened a small box in the back of the drawer and withdrew a wad of cash.

'Distribute it all,' I said.

'But, but, but,' stammered Lesley.

My glare told her not to keep talking or she would be on her way to Matron.

Lesley led a lonely life at the YWCA after that day with possibly her only true friendship being that of her pet rat.

I could not fathom where I got the strength to stand up to the bully Lesley. All through my high school teenage years I had been bullied. I was a timid country girl who was short in stature and slight in build. I had been made to feel inferior and small by many people in my life, but this had proved that when it really mattered in reality I did have an inner strength.

After these trying months card games seemed to wane in popularity so the board games became the entertainment on nights when television seemed a poor option. It was suggested that possibly an alcoholic drink may help many a dull night, but some wondered if that would all end badly as well, because the consequences if they were caught out did not bode well.

Secretly though many of the girls thought a drink or two might be a good idea and would certainly dull the pain of living in the over-regulated, boring and drab environment. Anything to spice life up a bit and send a bit of excitement through the place could not be all bad. Alcohol of any description was expensive, so there were only a limited number who could actually afford it, that is if they in reality wanted to partake.

I liked a bit of a drink myself and had been in trouble for drinking when I went to parties in my hometown. On one occasion my parents had sent me to a party to chaperone my older sister, Anne. My parents were not to know that they probably should not have entrusted this duty to me as both of us liked a drink and we both liked to party. I possibly drank more than Anne and I liked to mix my drinks, rum and coke, gin and tonic, vodka and orange, they were all enjoyed and of course they quickly went to my head and made me extremely tipsy. The teenagers of the small country town didn't find it difficult to obtain alcohol as the sons of the local pub owner would often come good after pilfering a decent amount of beverages from their fathers stock.

I should have known better, as one of the requests from my father was to look after my sister at a party, but I did the complete opposite. Thinking this was a perfect opportunity to party as hard as I could, but unfortunately for me, Anne left the party with a group of friends all who had consumed more than their fair share of alcohol. Country roads are not easy to navigate when one is sober let alone inebriated. The inevitable happened and there was a terrible accident in which Anne was seriously injured. She lost most of the skin off her back and had a serious injury to her arm. I discovered when my sister finally came home from hospital that I would be the primary carer, possibly punishment for my indiscretion in not looking after my sister at the party. As it transpired I did a pretty good job as Anne was dependent on me while the arm was encased in a metal contraption while it healed. I was very protective and would glare at people who stared at my sister and the medical aid that was attached to her arm. The first few weeks were a challenge as Anne was not as small as I was but she was dependant on me for her every need, even to turning her over in bed, not an easy task when the skin has been torn from your back and one arm doesn't work.

Even though all of this had an impact it was not enough to ward me off consuming alcohol. I was able to get my fair share especially as I got a little older and went to the dances at the Lyndale Town Hall. Once a month on a Friday night my mother would take Anne and I to Dandenong where she would sit with her best friend Betty while myself, Anne, and Betty's daughters, Cheryl and Sue would go to the dances. We saw many great bands including, Normie Rowe, Billy Thorpe and The Aztecs, Johnny O'Keefe, The Easybeats, Max Merritt, Bobby and Laurie, Ray Brown and The Whispers, Dinah Lee and The Groove. The entertainment was endless and every week there was a different band. These dances and the great Australian bands that were enjoyed was another reason that I was keen to go home for the weekend. The boys at the dances, that I got to know over time, would smuggle in small amounts of alcohol.

It would have been effortless and trouble free to smuggle alcohol in to the rooms at the YWCA as there was no such thing as bag checks. In fact, any sort of contraband one could procure that would fit in a bag was achievable. The only thing one didn't seem to be able to secretly deposit in one's room was a person of the male persuasion in the form of a boyfriend. The residents could come and go with whatever they liked in their bags. Getting caught was another matter though, as it was a strict rule that anyone caught drinking or with any evidence of imbibing would be instantly removed from the premises, never to return. It was imperative that no empty bottles be on display in the room and disposing of empty bottles in the bins was a no-no as that was tantamount to eviction immediately.

Matron could smell alcohol on a girl's breath from a mile away and as most girls were under the legal drinking age of 18, she was ever vigilant in the hope of catching out an unsuspecting 16 or 17-year-old. Surely she knew that if the girls were dating boys, many of whom were over 18 and had cars, then they were off to frequent many of the pubs in Richmond. Matron had such a radar she must have known that one of the favourite haunts was the Vaucluse in Swan Street.

During these times it came to light after the Lesley card games and the cheating that went on that Lesley always supplied a tipple for the girls. These refreshments she always supplied for the others to enjoy while she extracted as much money from them as she could. As the game progressed the cheating became more brazen. She was no dummy and knew that the alcohol would dull the senses of her fellow players, and they would become less vigilant and observant as the alcohol took effect.

The story was told by the card players that one night there was a knock on the door of Lesley's room when they were in the middle of a game.

'Quick, quick, down the hatch,' said Lesley through gritted teeth.

'Here, mints.' The mints were thrown across the bed.

As the door flung open Lesley deliberately knocked over the precious bottle of vodka and shoved the empty under the bed covers. As quick as a flash she removed some perfume from the dresser top to nullify the smell of alcohol.

'What is going on in here?' asked Matron.

'We are planning our next trip to the theatre,' exclaimed Lesley.

She was a dab hand with trickery and illusion, was Lesley as she had also managed to swiftly and expertly shove the cards under the bedspread that had been sitting on top of the pillow.

Matron knew something was amiss but what was it?

Lesley was one smart operator, prior to the gathering the vodka had been transferred from a genuine Smirnoff bottle to a plain bottle to put Matron off the trail of contraband.

'What is that you have spilt on the floor?' Matron demanded.

'Water,' replied Lesley.

'Clean it up,' growled Matron.

Lesley seemed to have all the answers and all bases covered as she was a chain smoker, and this seemed to mask the smell of the vodka. The mints appeared to do the job on the errant girls' bad breath.

'I am not sure what is really going on here,' barked Matron, 'but I will eventually get to the bottom of it.'

Lesley was one smooth operator who knew all the tricks of the trade. She was sly, dishonest and above all a blatant bully and therefore not to be crossed by anyone. There was not one girl at Doery House who had not been frightened of her, that was before the punishment muted out by the girls in relation to her cheating at cards and the threat to eradicate her pet rat.

The people in her care in her place of employment must have been frightened in to

subservience. It didn't bear thinking about.

Did the families of the patients in her care realise she was a bully and was probably using standover tactics on the patients at the home or hostel or hospital that she worked at?

It had been high time she had been put in place but the girls at the Y had only dealt with one part of her life. And they were concerned that even though they had managed to pull her in to line they wondered what was really happening to the people in her work life.

Was she punishing them because she wasn't ruling the world in her own home life? It didn't bear thinking about and sadly the residents of the YWCA were too young and were so consumed with their own world that they paid little attention to this issue.

18

DON'T MENTION THE WAR

Some of the girls at the YWCA took little interest in politics but then there were others who were passionate about what the present-day Government were planning, achieving and debating. In the latter half of the 1960s it appeared to be turbulent on the political front or so it seemed to me and all my young teenage friends.

One of the biggest issues was the Vietnam War and the protests from the youth of the day. My friends and I were extremely vocal with our opinions in relation to the situation; particularly heavy discussion took place at the dinner table in the evening. The National Service Scheme had been set up and the government were increasing the numbers that were conscripted. Whilst some thought this was okay there was a lot who didn't, particularly those girls who had teenage brothers who may be caught up in conscription. This was of particular concern when the numbers were increased, and many girls got trapped in the ideology and the vision of participating in the protests.

These types of subjects were best kept from Matron Lamrock as she would certainly inform us in no uncertain terms that the Vietnam War was of no concern to us. A lot of groups opposed National Service particularly the opposition in parliament (ALP), some religious organisations and particularly young guys and their families who may be affected. The member of the Labor Party who was most vocal was Jim Cairns; he seemed to lead an enormous movement against the Vietnam War. In fact, some said he may have been a good leader of the opposition or even a Prime Minister if he had focused more on main-stream politics. I didn't care which political persuasion he came from I just liked his message and his crusade as did so many other young people in Australia.

It was becoming apparent in late 1969 that public opposition to the Vietnam War had grown to such a degree that both main political parties recognised that the subject of the war could be a vote winner or kill off their chances of being elected. A whole generation of Australian young people were at last taking an interest in politics and the implications of major decisions made on their behalf.

Another group which also was gaining a voice was the Communist Party of Australia (CPA) but I knew rightly or wrongly that if I got involved with them it would be tantamount to my family divorcing me permanently, so I found out little about their direction and decided to steer clear, because no matter how much I wanted to participate and be a strong voice I also knew there was a line with my father that I could not cross.

Some of the Y girls, me included, were interested in

the Youth Campaign Against Conscription (YCAC). It had been formed in the mid-1960s and was gaining voice. I was very careful not to let on to my family that I was paying attention to them and wanted to get involved, after all they would tell me that I did not have any teenage brothers, and in fact the brother I did have was only born in 1966.

It seemed that a lot of Australians who had not been interested in politics, wars or even anti-war behaviour were becoming the key activists. There was also a group set up by middle class women called 'Save Our Sons'. I admired this group who had some of their faction participating in peaceful protests. These demonstrations were shown on the evening television news, highlighting to me how well dressed the women were, wearing their best clothes, their good shoes and their hats. Some even had their little children in prams along with them. These were not radical, unkempt troublemakers but passionate mothers, sisters, aunties and friends standing up for what they believed was right. They carried placards "How Long. How Many More", "Not With My Son You Don't", "Stop Bombing To Stop World War 3". There were posters around Melbourne and under a lot of the bridges showing a picture of war worn soldiers helping injured comrades and the words emblazoned 'Bring Them Home For Good'. Sydney started their protests before Melbourne which assisted with the momentum.

As well as television playing their part in conveying the atrocities of the war, newspapers had a large part in conveying the message along with swaying the thoughts of the reader in the direction and opinion of the reporter, journalist or editor. Some articles referred to the older generation supporting the involvement but in the minds of a lot of young people these were detached persons who did not have anyone directly affected in the conflict. There were a lot of stories perpetuated by a lot of different news outlets, politicians, academics and the like but my friends and I knew what the majority of the young people they associated with thought. A lot had their feelings in a quiet way, and it wasn't until the demonstrations, protests and finally the moratorium that many people had a combined voice.

I was aware though that the President of the USA was very popular in Australia and that over half a million people had welcomed his motorcade in 1966. The purpose of his visit was intended to show gratitude to Australia for their support of the Vietnam War. This visit was shortly after the Battle of Long Tan, between the Australian forces and the Viet Cong and North Vietnamese army units. There were some demonstrations associated with the visit but the full impact of what was happening in Vietnam and the treatment of the soldiers had not yet hit Australia. People had not fully realised they could express their point of view.

And what about the welfare and the wellbeing of the Vietnamese people, the footage on television was the stuff of nightmares to a lot of the residents at the Y?

These people did not want to be involved.

Secretly I started to make contact with YCAC. I was ready to make a difference and discovered that there were others at Doery House willing to partake as well. Over 60,000 young guys, sons, brothers, nephews and friends had already gone to war as the conflict in Vietnam dragged on. So many young men received the 'short straw' when their birth date was randomly chosen, and they later received their conscription documentation in the mail. All guys at the age of twenty were compelled to register with the government but the government did not want everyone to go so that is how the ballot came about.

After all, how would the country survive if every male aged twenty went off to war to fight?

At that time Australia was considered to have tantamount to full employment. It seemed like a lottery to many in the reverse, because a lottery should have a lucky outcome not a negative result.

They were bitterly disappointed when one of the most popular singers of the 1960's, Normie Rowe was inducted into the army in 1968 and sent to fight in Vietnam in 1969 after he was drafted for National Service.

Like so many people I started to encourage the boys I knew, either directly or indirectly, to fight back and destroy their documents even though they were breaking the law. These dissidents were classed as dangerous and a menace, but they were the ones who helped pick up the momentum for the first moratorium to take place in 1970.

A moratorium was held in America in 1969 and a lot of the girls took notice of this and wondered why Australia was not rallying together quicker. A wave was slowly gathering in to a tsunami though and the people would be heard. A change was taking place and I felt I was a small part of this movement. I would talk to anyone and everyone about it with the exception of my family. It was common knowledge that agitators could be in serious trouble and that some were sent to prison if they resisted conscription.

Another reason it was imperative that my family did not get a hint of what I was doing was the fact that my family were Liberal Party voters to the core of their bones. They looked on any person who was not of their political persuasion as some kind of intellectual failure and who couldn't possibly have the best interests of Australia foremost in their thoughts. In fact, they probably looked down on anyone who was not a devotee of the Liberal Party.

Clandestine meetings were set-up, knowing that if they were caught out or their purpose was discovered they would be immediately evicted from Doery House. Any type of radical or unusual behaviour would not be tolerated.

One of the heart-breaking occurrences was that the anti-war attitude became such a force that some of the public were treating returned soldiers as if they were at fault rather than the very government that had put conscription in to place. It was so rampant that soldiers were advised not to tell anyone, outside their immediate family, what they had been doing in their life recently. A group of my friends saw a particularly bad incident where returned soldiers were abused, had rotten eggs and tomatoes thrown at them and were literally made to feel like they were the scum of the earth.

One newspaper in Melbourne that broke stories about Vietnam veterans and Agent Orange was 'Truth'. It was a tabloid newspaper that often-published stories that no other paper wanted or knew about. They also liked to publish scandalous stories and articles relating to social injustice. It was the paper to read in relation to those unfortunate persons who had landed in trouble with the law, with many court and police reports published. Many Melbournians loved to read 'Truth' but few would readily admit to it. One of my sisters went on to date with a reporter from the paper. My father was particularly happy about this at it meant he would get a complimentary edition each week. My mother forbade her daughters from reading it, but this did not stop us as the stories contained within were of the likes we had not been exposed to in the past and they certainly made entertaining reading.

The death of the Prime Minister, Harold Holt, on Sunday 17 December 1967, was a national shock and tragedy to most Australians. I had it implanted in my brain at the time and for the rest of my life. My family went regularly to our holiday home at Loch Sport on the Gippsland Lakes. We usually arrived for the weekend on either the Friday night or the Saturday morning and departed for the homeward journey on the Sunday late in the afternoon.

I did not particularly enjoy all of the time spent at Loch Sport, due to the fact that I was an asthmatic and there seemed to be a mosquito invasion every time we visited Loch Sport. To exterminate or discourage the pesky mosquitoes my mother and father set up a mass wall of mosquito coils, which subsequently played havoc with my asthma. I wheezed all night and was particularly grumpy when the sun came up each morning through sheer exhaustion and the need to get away from those irritating mosquito coils.

My father had a boat which was his pride and joy and was one of the pluses for visiting lots of interesting spots on the Gippsland Lakes. There was always some exciting place to travel to and then to pull the boat into for a picnic and a swim. I was not really what one would call a beach bikini type of girl, but I did enjoy the trips in the boat.

On one of these particular visits to Loch Sport we were journeying home and had just stopped at the regular take away that served delicious, unhealthy, fatty, salty, not very good food when they heard the terrible news. I was not actually seated in the car as anyone who purchased a chiko roll, which I and my sisters often did, had to leave the car while the delicious roll of dubious ingredients was in their possession. My father flatly refused to have anyone in the car eating chiko rolls although for some reason all the other absolutely, not very good food was allowed particularly fish and chips. Maybe my father couldn't stand the smell of fifth time cooked cabbage.

While the sisters were standing outside the back-passenger door my father all of a sudden yelled, 'Get back in the car, Harold Holt is missing.'

My sisters and I looked at each other exclaiming, 'But what are we supposed to do with our chiko rolls?'

The Prime Minister seemed old to me as a teenager, but I quickly learnt that he was still a young man who considered himself fit and healthy. He died while swimming at Cheviot Beach near Portsea in Victoria. His body was never found. It was his routine pattern everyone was told; he loved the surf and he loved to swim. He had a great knowledge of the beach, but rip tides and rough seas are no match for any man. Everyone wondered what would happen as he was pro-Vietnam when he won the election in 1966. His short-term predecessor was John McEwen and then shortly afterwards John Gorton became Prime Minister. So, in the time I was at Doery House there were three prime ministers all from the Liberal Party.

Along with the Vietnam War and all its intricacies and then the disappearance of Harold Holt there was also many other issues that were of interest to the young girls at the YWCA.

At last Indigenous people were to be counted in the census.

Why weren't they counted in the past, aren't they people who live in Australia like everyone else?

And a year later the Indigenous were to get full wages on pastoral stations. This was another matter that the girls found very strange in relation to the length of its implementation.

The introduction of decimal currency in 1966 was an enormous change to people's lives. The young embraced it and the elderly opposed it with all their might.

A top security space facility was established at Pine Gap near Alice Springs in the Northern Territory. The girls at the Y wanted pictures as it sounded exciting but unfortunately they were not forthcoming.

At last in 1969 after decades of campaigning women workers were granted equal pay rates with men doing comparable work. Most of the girls at the Y laughed at this suggestion as they knew the chances of this happening were pretty remote. The other matter was how many men actually did the jobs that the females were employed doing. After much discussion the girls calculated it was probably close to 5 percent of the girls who resided at the Y actually knew a male who was or would be employed in a similar job to their own.

The most exciting news, for many around the world was in 1969 when men landed on the moon. It was reported that millions of people around the world watched it take place with the images being seen on television. The images were received from the space module, Apollo 11, via Australia's giant telescope in Parkes, New South Wales. They were all very animated on seeing the erection of the United States flag on the moon's surface. All the residents at the Y were very excited seeing it on television and they couldn't get enough of the words, "The Eagle has landed" and "That's one small step for man, one giant leap for mankind".

19

SÉANCES

There was far too much time to while away at the hostel. After dinner or tea many of the girls had to find a means to fill in idle moments, the need to amuse themselves was never ending. They were teenagers with boundless amounts of energy and plenty of high spirits; they had plenty of time that could be put to good use or a way to get up to no good. They wanted to make each other laugh, entertain and be entertained.

There was only so much television one could watch, and the choices were limited, the thought of sitting in the uncomfortable television room chairs also discouraged many residents from that means of using free moments. The time in the evening was soul destroying for many, they were lonely, some had few friends in the city environment which they were unfamiliar with, and they were missing their families. Those who smoked were also not appreciated by those who were non-smokers. As I was an asthmatic I was happy to retreat to the sewing room where I set the rules. Smoking was strictly forbidden around the dressmaking.

Some girls went out in the evening, while others played cards ignoring the possibility that they were running the risk of being caught, whilst others secretly drank away their cares and woes.

Debbie arrived in the middle of 1969 and it was evident from the start that she was up for a good time and was not about to let boredom overcome her. She was a refreshing change and often had mealtime in an uproar with her anecdotes and tales from her hometown in country Victoria.

Debbie sparked interest in acquiring knowledge on the possibility that someone had died at Doery House during its existence. One couldn't ask the matron as she would not be impressed and probably wouldn't know if someone had shuffled off the earth at 353 Church Street. Debbie had a brilliant idea, well in her mind anyway. She could hold a séance. This way she was sure they could all discover whether the place had seen anybody leave in a box, as she put it.

Séances were fashionable with a group of people wanting to visit a medium or hoping to see objects levitate or hear the voices of those who had departed the earth. Maybe they could communicate with the spirits, maybe they could receive messages from ghosts, or they could listen to a medium then relay messages back. Was it all magic, maybe it was all in the mind or possibly it was true?

After a lot of discussion and planning a date was set up for the first séance. Debbie went to the Melbourne public library to research all she could on the topic. After all, if she was going to lead the group she would need to be in full control and appear to know what she was doing and what direction the group was going even if it was not the case.

While trying to study up on this spooky idea she came across all sorts of information on Ouija boards or spirit boards, but where was she going to get one of these flat pieces of timber? Masonite or chipboard would be good but once again where was she going to get that and even if she did manage to acquire one, how was she going to get it back to Doery House. She did not have a car and neither did any of the other residents.

No one seemed to be sure if this was a rule or was it just the fact that most of the girls were too young to have a driver's licence?

Even if Debbie or any of the other residents did have a car, it would not be practical at the YWCA as there was no car park. Leaving a vehicle in the street overnight was not a good idea either as trams and cars played dodgems all through the night in Church Street. It was never discussed and did not seem to concern the girls as most of them were under eighteen years of age anyway.

And besides where would any of them get the money for a car as the YWCA managed to keep the residents penniless by charging them high rent that left the majority of girls with very little spare cash?

Debbie hatched a plan to get the Ouija board, but she knew she would have to lie to her father, her uncle or her brother. One of them had to be told that she needed the timber for a project she was completing. The other consideration was the need for one of them to deliver it to the YWCA preferably without Matron in attendance when it arrived. Debbie thought her uncle was the best choice as he would ask fewer questions and surprisingly her plan went without a hitch. She even managed to smuggle the masonite in to her room without another soul seeing her. Her uncle helped her plan everything with little fuss and questioning. She knew that she could hide the newly acquired Ouija board behind the wardrobe and the chances of the house cleaner seeing it were very remote. In fact, the cleaning outside the dining room seemed to be hit and miss, more miss than hit. Maria was the housekeeper and kitchen hand, and it appeared that she needed help, and a lot of it, if she was going to make an impression on the enormous building. She was a large lady who lumbered around behind the equally well-endowed cook, with her long-plaited hair, twirled on the top of her head. There was a lot of duster waving and broom swinging but little headway was made, particularly on the masses of timber floors throughout the whole building.

The bathrooms, mostly made of concrete, received little attention as how did one clean concrete walls?

Debbie decorated the Ouija board with symbols, some letters and numbers as she had seen in diagrams in the books she had read at the library.

The first group to attend the inaugural séance meeting consisted of Maureen, Claire, Kathy, Linda, Sylvia and of course, Debbie. They all thought it would be a bit of a laugh, but some did not feel that way by the end of this get together. In fact, a couple of the girls were terrified and thought the building was haunted. Other girls felt the mediums offered them wellbeing and esotericism in a gloomy world. Of course, there were also some who saw through Debbie and believed it was all trickery and knew it was fake. They had a bit of fun with it as well, even with the knowledge that they were exploiting the vulnerable, which was cruel as some of the partakers were barely fifteen years old. Word quickly got around though and there was rapidly becoming the need for a waiting list, as many girls wanted to join in.

Debbie had what most discovered later a blossoming theatrical talent that somehow developed into a wonderful penchant for illusion. She managed to convince many a girl that the Ouija board and the smaller board that was the pointer were moving on their own when actually it was the person using the board who was unknowingly doing the guiding.

Debbie even managed, by switching off the bedroom light and only having a weak torchlight, to create an eerie setting which induced the participants into believing that the table was levitating when in actual fact it remained stationery. She had accomplished the ultimate persona of the subconscious mind as described in her readings. Some of the girls described the feelings as a paranormal phenomenon.

Debbie had chosen her first meeting time well as it was the night before Halloween. She informed one and all she was going to contact the spirit world, she wanted all the girls to hold hands around the table, and much to the astonishment of all she got a reply, well that is what it seemed. Debbie had a tête-à-tête with a ghost. She thought this was all a bit of a laugh even though she kept on her serious face throughout her chat with the ghost. Some girls started seeing and hearing weird things at the Y after this meeting even though there had not been any reports of anything untoward until Debbie started her séances. All agreed though that this was a friendly spirit and not to be feared.

Debbie became adept at creating the illusion that the smaller board on top of the Oujia board was spelling words from the letters that she had drawn on top of the mainboard. She became so skilful at scaring the living daylights out of the residents, but still the girls kept queuing up to be a part of this spiritual experience.

Sadly, this bit of frivolity did not last as Debbie left shortly before Christmas never to be seen again. Her roommate announced the Oujia board was still behind the wardrobe and did anyone wish to take up Debbie's mantle but there were no takers. It appeared that all and sundry wanted to leave séances in the past. It was agreed by all that Debbie had lightened the evening dullness at Doery House, even if only for a short time.

20

ETIQUETTE GONE MAD

One got the impression that Matron thought a large proportion of the girls were ill-mannered, unladylike, unpresentable, some bordering on impolite, others discourteous and possibly even badly brought up. Her solution to the problem was going to be classes conducted by her that would cover the way young ladies should carry themselves when they dined out. She would deliver to the residents a lesson in table manners like no other. She would also educate us in the art of conversation and the correct use of telephones. Of course, etiquette would be covered in all forms. Most of the girls were from the country and had varying levels of socially correct behaviour. Refinement and grace, polish and sophistication had not been high on the list of priorities for a lot of country folk. I agreed that some were a bit rough around the edges but wasn't that life.

Many of the girls at the Y decided that as life was sometimes dull after dinner that Matron could spice it up with all her knowledge. As she had never been married and as we girls couldn't imagine any man wanting to go out to dinner with her we all imagined the series of five evenings could be a bit of a laugh and at least it was better than watching reruns on the television.

The first night was titled 'Dining Out'

All the girls were shocked at some of the rules –

The woman follows the waiter and waits to be seated. If there is no waiter, the woman follows the man. (All good so far)

Glasses, keys, handbags and personal items should be placed on the floor or on one's lap. (Not a good idea to place all those items on your lap, what about the table if there is room?)

Place table napkin on lap once seated, if the waiter does not do this then you should.

Don't tuck your napkin into your collar. (The participants wondered who would do this, they giggled and thought this was what old people would do)

If asked a question while you have food in your mouth, you can discreetly bring your napkin to your lips to show you are unable to reply.

The man asks the woman what she would like and orders for both, the ladies choices first (Goodness, can't girls talk for themselves?)

Don't rest elbows on the table.

Keep each mouthful small.

Don't chew with your mouth open.

Don't talk when you have food in your mouth.

Don't speak loudly or shout at the table.

Don't mash or stir all your food together.

Taste food before adding salt and pepper.

Don't turn your fork over to scoop up peas etc.

Do not hold your knife as if it was a pen or pencil.

Do not eat too fast, this is vulgar, but do not eat too slow as all others will have to wait for you to finish. (It seemed that eating out was somewhat complicated)

Don't use your utensils to serve yourself from a serving dish. (Who would actually do this?)

Do not smoke while someone at the table is eating. (Don't smoke at all as it wrecks the food for everyone in the restaurant)

If you accidently drop your cutlery, ask the man to request the waiter to bring clean ones.

Never blow on food to cool it down.

Good table manners are silent table manners. (This obviously wasn't practiced at Doery House)

Never dunk food in your drinks.

*Pick up your wine glass by the stem (*We all thought this was a recipe for disaster*)*

Don't point with your cutlery.

Don't pick your teeth with your fingernail.

Don't announce to all and sundry that you are going to the toilet, just stand and say, 'excuse me'.

Only hold your cutlery when you are cutting food.

Put your cutlery on the plate while you are chewing.

Don't hand your plate to the waiter.

Don't crumble your napkin when finished and place on your plate but rather fold it and leave it to the left of your plate.

When finished, leave your plate in front of you, never push it away.

Smile

Matron informed us at the end of the session that if

we followed all her teachings on dining then we would not deny others the opportunity of enjoying their meal. Consideration for others and avoiding transgressions would make a good impression of our behaviour and therefore we would be welcome at any dinner table be it with a male companion, a friend, a work colleague or a family member. Matron told us if we got the hiccups during a meal we were not to apologise as it would only draw attention to the problem. She didn't inform us on the best remedy to eliminate them forthwith.

That was the first night for all of the residents who took part at the hostel. We agreed that we didn't mind these life skill lessons as it gave us something to practice at mealtimes, and more importantly something to giggle about and then to dissect every little rule. Some commented that the funniest one was to smile, as it would be difficult before becoming well practiced in remembering all the rules and regulations to actually smile. There was also lots of chatter about neither eating too fast nor too slow. I felt my father would approve of this as he ate very fast and my mother ate slowly.

The second week the subject was 'The Art of Conversation'

The topic of conversation should be cheerful and interesting. If having dinner where conversation is a part then cheerful conversation would aid digestion. (Matron was unable to tell us medically or scientifically how this would come about)

Stay away from thoughtless and inappropriate

conversational topics. (How was one supposed to know what they were?)

Converse in subjects of mutual interest. (How would we know the topics that were of interest to both parties if you had only just met?)

Do not bore people with a subject that they are showing obvious disinterest in. If the subject they are discussing is boring you then discreetly change the subject.

To enable you to have interesting topics of conversation you need to listen to other people carefully and to take in all you see and read.

Do not answer questions with one liners or a simple 'yes' or 'no'.

Watch people's faces when you are talking, and you will know if the subject is interesting to them or the complete reverse.

If someone begins to look away or show signs of a lack of concentration you would be a wise conversationalist if you tastefully changed the subject.

We sat around the television room having our supper of dry cracker biscuits along with the plain cake drizzled with pink icing and coconut sprinkled on top discussing the night's topic. The cheap powdery hot chocolate, which was not anything like our mothers would make, helped to dilute the dry supper. We found this particular evening amusing as Matron's strong point in her character was not conversation.

She talked at the residents not with them, and surely she could see most of her subjects were not in the least bit interesting to the residents, but did she change the subject or allow us to vary the topic to something we would like to discuss?

She certainly did not practice what she preached. We wondered if anything she had taught us in two weeks had actually been put in to practice in her life. Next week was something to look forward to as there wasn't much else at Doery House to dream about or wait expectantly to happen.

The third night the residents at the Y got together the topic was 'Telephones'

Introduce yourself when you make a call. Don't automatically assume people know who you are by the sound of your voice.

Remember that you speak "with" people not "to" people.

When you make a call identify yourself to the recipient and if you know them don't forget to use their name.

If you find that the person on the other end of the phone speaks very loudly it could be a message that you are speaking too softly.

If you are taking a message for someone else ask the caller for their name.

Don't speak abruptly on the phone.

By the end of this evening we were pretty bored and felt that they had been given information that they already knew. Telephones were something we were all used to and after all many of us had to make and receive calls at our workplace. At the hostel there was always the constant battle of avoiding the phone at

Doery House due to the fact that sometimes it was almost impossible to find the recipient in the 'rabbit warrens' of the building.

'Don't yell,' Matron would boom as one was looking for the girlfriend of a star struck lover on the end of the phone. It mustn't have been very pleasant for the person on the end of the phone to hear the screaming girls but there really was no alternative. Family members seemed to be a little more forgiving and would often ask if you could try again if their daughter, sister, grand-daughter or niece could not be found on the first try. New residents quickly learnt to avoid the telephone cubicle area at all costs. Unfortunately, if one was waiting for a call you often got caught up in having to answer an incoming call and then having to run around to find the recipient. There was a buzzer for those girls who had rooms upstairs but the major problem with this system was that no one upstairs would actually respond to the buzzer. The good-natured person who answered the original call now had a double amount of heartache as they had to wait for the call to finish before they could receive their anticipated call. There were only two lines into the building and many outside callers gave up in despair after trying many times to reach their loved ones. Most girls on receiving a call from a friend or family member would not observe the ruling given for a limit of 10 minutes per phone call. There was one line out which was primarily used by the girls to reverse the charges on the long-distance calls to their parents. Most of the residents did not know anyone in Melbourne and the surrounding suburbs so they did not want to feed coins into that contraption which to them was more like a slot machine than a telephone. If they did use coins many a girl got cut off in the middle of a private or personal call when the money ran out.

Telephone etiquette was sorely tried in these times.

The fourth and thankfully second last session was 'Introductions'

Use the person's name and the words 'I would like you to meet'. Do not use 'this is'.

Try to use surnames. (This seemed awfully formal as most of the girls at Doery House didn't actually know anyone's surnames)

Mention the name of the most important person first. (Didn't everyone think they were important? How was one supposed to gauge who was the most important?)

Stand up when you are being introduced to someone.

Don't introduce your parents as 'Mum and Dad'. They have names.

Repeat the name when introduced so that it is set in your memory. Remember names. Make a point of actively listening.

This evening also was basic and the best part for all of us was that we only had one more session to go. At supper that night we had great fun mimicking matron and attempting some role play of introductions with the girls in the television room. We had to be careful as it would not be a great thing if matron heard us making fun of her and her classes.

At last the final night had arrived and the topic was 'Etiquette'.

The basis of good manners is to be super thoughtful to other people. Awareness of others is key.

If anyone offers to shake hands then do so, even if it is another female. Do not shake hands with a limp wrist.

If men stand when you enter the room either sit down quickly or ask them to be seated.

Allow a man to walk downstairs first and to have him walk on the outside on a footpath.

Women walk first through a doorway, but a man should lead the way through a crowd of people.

Women should wait for a man to open the door.

Don't be pushy.

Don't head for the biggest and best chair in someone's lounge room.

Don't fiddle with the lighting.

Don't put your feet up on the furniture, even if it is obviously a foot stool.

Do not place a glass on a piece of polished furniture in case it leaves a mark.

Care for others in everything you do.

We were intrigued that matron had used the words 'super thoughtful', as we did not particularly believe that matron had been very thoughtful to anyone in all the time they had been residents at the Y, let alone her being super thoughtful.

Imagine a man standing when you entered a room. We all agreed that we could not wait for this to happen, if ever it did.

When we were all back in the television room having the watery hot chocolate and the passable fruit cake we admitted it had been a bit of a hoot. Everyone agreed it had been enjoyable and a way to fill in 5 nights at the hostel. Matron had taken it all so seriously and was not able to find one single item that could give most of us a small smile let alone a laugh. The residents at the Y were chastised if there was even the slightest snigger which only made them laugh more.

21

MELTING POT OF FAITHS

My family had a strong religious background, first as a member of the Church of England and then as a member of the Anglican Church of Australia.

My family had deep roots with my Great Grandfather being the builder of the small timber church in Upper Beaconsfield. My family and all my descendants were very proud of this fact.

I can recall attending Sunday School each and every Sunday in the local hall. At the end my friends and I would all walk down the hill to the church to greet our parents as they were being farewelled at the church door by the Vicar. As I became a teenager I also assumed the role of a Sunday School teacher which continued in my years at the YWCA.

My parents attended church every week. When my father bought a magnificent car called a Humber Super Snipe it would be positioned at the back of the church on Sundays right next to the park allocated for the Vicar, but when the Archbishop of Melbourne came to visit then he would take the Vicar's car park. This was all done in a very measured way by my father as the Archbishop also had a Humber Super Snipe and he had a chauffeur which made the whole theatrics of the event even more stunning for my father.

The Archbishop of Melbourne had a holiday house in my hometown, so the Archbishop was a regular visitor. The town folk welcomed him and enjoyed his company. Archbishop Frank Woods was a charming man, tall and handsome. His wife always welcomed any visitors with warmth and open arms. I remember myself and my older sister playing with the Archbishop's daughter Clemie when they visited. Clemie was very good at tennis.

Many of the girls who resided at the Y went to church on a regular basis whether they went home each weekend or whether they stayed at Doery House.

I saw evidence of the numbers who went to church by just looking at St. Ignatius Catholic Church that was opposite the YWCA. There seemed to be a service of some kind every day and Church Street was jammed with parishioners all heading in the one direction. Parking spaces for cars were at a premium.

There seemed to be so many strong beliefs around in the 1960s and there appeared to be some organisation at every corner ready to tap into those beliefs and endeavouring to change the way young vulnerable people thought.

One such organisation was the Hare Krishna Movement. They were prominent in many locations around Melbourne. Many teenage girls and boys were fascinated by the chanting and dancing of the men and women in their saffron robes, many sporting shaved heads. Many of the girls from the YWCA were enchanted in varying degrees by the way they appeared to be spreading peace and understanding in a haze of incense or some other concoction. They collected donations for the food that they cooked to be distributed to the believers and the needy.

I was indeed mesmerized by them when I came across them in the centre of Melbourne. In fact, one was more likely to hear them before they were apparent to the eye. I did not at any time have any spare money to place in their donation bowl but I had been warned by others to be wary of this act of kindness because it was a sign to the Hare Krishna's that you were sympathetic to their causes and you may be a valuable candidate to coax in to their movement.

They would also hand out booklets spreading the word about their virtues, and also their beliefs about gambling, drugs and vegetarians.

There was one very scary cult group that the girls regularly talked about called The Manson Family. Charles Manson was the leader and they had a big commune in the USA. The residents at the Y seemed to question why most of his followers were females. He convinced many of his followers to commit terrible crimes including murder.

The residents of Doery House were certainly conscious of these outside 'so-called' religions or cults but were smart enough not to be caught up in their followings other than to be mindful of their attraction to some.

The religions that were at the forefront of the majority of the girls were Catholic, Anglican (Church of England), Methodists, Presbyterian and Baptist. Many girls practised their faith and went to church on Sundays.

One resident at the YWCA was a Jehovah's Witness but for reasons unknown to her fellow dwellers she refused to talk about the teachings and beliefs. I remember my father coming home from the local hotel when he had been fund-raising for the local Country Fire Authority with the Jehovah's Witness magazine 'The WatchTower'. From this I imagined that this religion was not averse to endeavouring to increase its flock by visiting the local pub.

22

THE REUNION

Would they come? To call a reunion was a brave thing as although some may have happy memories certainly those from the late 1960s would have mixed feelings and memories. The friendships built may be lasting that had been built on comradeship and a strong sense of survival in what was at times a harsh environment in which to live, but they also may be memories that some would not want to relive. Old wounds may be opened that didn't have the benefit of young healing powers and the many diversions they brought of friends, marriage, children, a career, family, travel and as was said in the song 'life is what happens when you are busy making other plans'. A reunion would be a risky event to organise, but one would never know unless you plunged in and embraced the response no matter how small or how grand.

I need not have worried as they came from far and wide and the stories told were heartbreaking, joyous, alarming, spirited, touching and everything in between.

Those who came were not just residents from the late 1960s as many were in their seventies and eighties who had been at Doery House in the '40s and '50s, they came along with family members of past residents and even some of the boyfriends of the girls from the

YWCA.

After all these years and so much planning it was truly amazing to see them all coming in droves. There had been many who had responded in the affirmative to the invitation, there had been much enthusiasm, there had been offers of assistance, and the tidal wave of positivity had at times been overwhelming.

There were stories and memories from Janice, Janet, Wendy, Judy, Marjorie, Glenys, Joy, Patsy, Chrissie, Carol, Moira, Sue, Noela, Lorna, Marie, Heather, Cheryl, Dusty, Alice, Lois, Liz, Elizabeth, Marian, Candy, Coralie, Helen, Maureen, Claire, Erica, Kathy, Linda, Sylvia, Annette, Susan, Gayle, Jean, Mavis, June, Betty and so many others. The boyfriends from those days who were brave enough to come along and even recount stories of others were Billy, Peter, Jim, Ribs, John, Keith, Barry, Eric, Greg, Lenny, Ray, Tony and David. I will be forever grateful to all of them for their contributions and memories of the days at Doery House in the late 1960s.

And the years that spanned all these girls who were now women, ladies and mature girls really were incredible. The oldest resident with recollections was 96 and the youngest was 65. The memory retention for some was fading while others could recall happenings of yesteryear in Richmond like it was last week.

They were quite happy to expose the details of their town or origin when they arrived at the YWCA in Richmond. Most had never ventured outside the small townships they had spent their childhood, after all they were still children, albeit teenagers when they arrived at Doery House. Hearts and souls of places from faraway had filled the rooms of the hostel with girls looking for a home away from home as they started their working lives. Homes conjure up impressions of families, warmth and love but unfortunately that was not the case for many who ventured through that wire gate at the beginning of the cracked concrete path that led to the wooden door of the construction that was often just a building. A home is viewed as a place of peace, a sanctuary from all the doubt and division outside. If the anxieties of the outer life penetrate it then it just becomes somewhere to lay your head.

Towns that are familiar now would have been foreign to many of the girls as they had ventured little from their isolated country towns: Foster, Yarram, Mornington, Cranbourne, Simpson, Caramut, Warrnambool, Upper Beaconsfield, Colac, Mt. Beauty, Wodonga, Ararat, Lake Boga, The Riverina, Bairnsdale, Leongatha, Newborough, Wesburn, Inglewood, Moe, Swan Hill, Eildon, Warburton, King Island, Flinders Island and even from as far away as Adelaide.

The common theme was the need for the parents of the residents to ensure their daughter was housed in a safe and secure environment, which provided warmth and nourishment. The harsh reality was often far from what had been promised or anticipated.

After the initial reservations and shyness, the chatter about times past increased dramatically. For some of the attendees walking into the gathering was intimidating to say the least but it didn't take too long for an enormous outpouring of stories, history and information. Many in attendance found comrades they had not set eyes on for over fifty years.

How wonderful to see so many mates come along, many had been boyfriends or just friends of the girls who lived at the hostel, some had remained friends, some had even married the great love they had discovered while living at Doery House.

Sadly, a common theme appeared that a large proportion of the girls did not find love everlasting, whether it first blossomed from these days at the Y or not. Many marriages faltered and divorce was imminent. In fact, I found it quite confronting that such a large proportion of marriages had not survived.

Could it have possibly been anything to do with the time spent in their formative teenage years? Was there a higher percentage of divorce from the Y girls than in the general population?

No one would ever know, although it was difficult at the gathering to find someone who was still in their first marriage. Some girls were in their third or fourth relationship. Many girls had sad tales to impart in relation to their love lives.

Conversation turned to many topics, friendships, relationships, rules and regulations, hardships, loneliness, depression, the matron, the hours, the extreme temperature changes, and the living conditions but the main topic of dialogue centred on the food including the quallty, quantity and variety. Most, if not all, had thoughts of the food being of the same or similar quality to that which they had experienced through their childhood in family life. What a shock they had experienced. This was discussed in great length; the gluggy custard, the lumpy gravy that was often congealed, the morning cup of tea arriving in the big battered aluminium teapot that had been allowed to brew and stew for more time than any tea grower or tea producer had ever contemplated.

The bread was never fresh but would have made perfect breadcrumbs or acceptable food for the birds, as it was of the correct degree of staleness. Maybe the cook got the bread cheap if she relieved the baker of the stale loaves or maybe the Y bought in such enormous quantities that by the time the girls were expected to consume it then it had seen better days, or possibly the fresh bread was reserved exclusively for the staff. By the size of them all it appeared they had nibbled on a sandwich or two. Possibly 3 or 4 slices of toast with marmalade for breakfast and at the end of the day a slice or two with dinner for the staff. None of the girls can ever remember bread being baked on the premises. Bread was served at dinner as well as breakfast and although it was always stale many girls partook as when one is hungry then even stale bread with a thick spread of butter can be made palatable. Always at the ready was a large glass of water or a mug of tea to wash it down with.

Some of the girls referred to the food offerings as basic, ordinary and some other unkind descriptions.

Many said mealtime made them hanker for their home life even more, as generally speaking country mothers were wonderful in the kitchen serving lots of comfort food made with plenty of love which would indeed make everyone happy. The girls who were at the YWCA in the 1950s recounted the food as being adequate, but as the meaning of adequate is often likened to tolerable, sufficient or fair then the standard was somewhat dubious. The girls from the 1960s did not have such a high opinion but possibly the cooks were not as competent or maybe the funds they had been allocated to purchase food to provide for the girls had been reduced over the years.

There were plenty of places to purchase a snack if one was hungry and had the funds to venture to the milk bar, sadly I wasn't one of them, having such little money that it was barely enough to exist on. The girls told a story of trips to the local shops over the years to acquire food that they felt was more edible than that served at the Y. There was the Black Swan Coffee Shop in Church Street, Chris's Italian Coffee Shop, The International Coffee Bar, Bob's Hamburger Bar in Bridge Road, The Tiger Milk Bar (owned by former Richmond Football great, Jack Dyer) also in Church Street.

Strangely not one of the girls mentioned attending the football at the Melbourne Cricket Ground.

There were stories about pots and pans being taken the Gold and Well Chinese restaurant in Swan Street to be filled up with their favourite food which happened to be chicken chow mien. The other Chinese shop that served good food was Wing Wah in Bridge Road.

The oldest person who came was Marjorie and at 96 years of age she looked amazing. Marjorie said her memory was fading but who could blame her as she was born in 1922 and she was at the YWCA in Richmond for four years from the age of 17 to 21. When prompted she really did remember quite a substantial amount about her years at the hostel. She was well educated and continued in that vein for many years. She was a boarder at Methodist Ladies College and matriculated there having then gone on to train as a radiographer. Marjorie managed to get her qualifications by going by tram to night school in the city. She was employed by Dr Thomas in the Hospital x-ray department in Bridge Road. She clearly remembered that she x-rayed the knees of Joan Sutherland and was duly given tickets for her and her mother to see Joan Sutherland perform in Melbourne. Marjorie remembered that four years was the maximum one could stay at Doery House and that the hierarchy were particular about the exit of a resident once the age of 21 years was reached. You were 'cast out, had to look after yourself and find other accommodation', she recalled.

Marjorie had a room in the main building and her roommate slept on the balcony every night as this was all she could afford. I felt maybe I hadn't been so badly done by after all as I had only had to sleep on the balcony every second week. Marjorie's roommate had a cupboard in her room to house her belongings. Marjorie felt it was her responsibility to look after the cupboard by keeping the door to her room locked, as she knew that the old, dilapidated container was a poor excuse for storing one's clothing.

Marjorie did not think the food was too disagreeable and she also did not believe the rules and regulations were too strict as she had come from a solid religious Methodist home and had been to boarding school so she felt she adapted well. But in saying that she recognised it was difficult for some girls who had lived a sheltered life in the country with their families, and with little exposure to city life.

Marjorie played the piano and remembered an annual celebration around the Christmas period with all the girls singing along.

Marjorie's brother lived in a flat behind the St. Ignatius Church, which was opposite the hostel in Church Street. Marjorie was happy about this as she was able to see him regularly and they could journey together when travelling to see her parents in Inglewood, north west of Melbourne. She remembered her mother being in the Country Women's Association. She didn't go home regularly at weekends as it was a long trip. When travelling around the city she would use the tram as she preferred it to train travel.

The boiler room was stoked with coke to supply the hot water for Doery House. It was expected that if you walked past the boiler room you shovelled a shovel of coke under the boiler. While most girls didn't like this chore they also did not like the prospect of not having a supply of hot water. Marjorie remembered frequently completing this chore and often ending up with coke dust on her skin and/or clothes.

When washing her clothes at Doery House in the old copper Marjorie would also attend to her brother's washing. In those days it was not expected that a male would complete his own washing and as they lived so close Marjorie took it upon herself to do the laundry.

Marjorie frequently went to dances. She recalled that every night the closing time was 11.30pm except for Saturday when it was 12 midnight. She liked dating boys and remembered most boys being 'gentlemen'. She didn't marry until the age of 35 and that marriage only lasted 8 years. She did not have children and never remarried.

If one missed the closing time for the front door at Doery House the resident would go to the door on the Southside of the building, tap on the window of another sympathetic and friendly resident who would then let them in by the fire escape door which was never permanently locked. I wondered when the rules and regulations changed to the dangerous practice of having the fire escape doors permanently locked. With the passing of time it seems an absolute miracle that there was not a catastrophic accident at the YWCA hostel in Richmond.

Olive was in her early 80s and she distinctly

remembered one night in October 1953 when two armed robbers wearing face coverings, that she thought may have been small scarves or handkerchiefs, held up the YWCA hostel. They stormed in through the front door and demanded money from Matron Walters and Matron Gordon. One of the matrons retrieved the money from the money tin and threw it all in the air but the two men clambered around all through the office to recover the notes. The police were called, and it was a great story for the girls to tell their work colleagues the next day and their family on the weekend.

Betty was another ex-resident who at 90 years of age also looked incredible and was happy to tell all her wonderful and thought-provoking stories. Her memory was sharp in relation to her days at the YWCA. She lived at the Y in 1947 when she was 17 years old. It appears that like Marjorie she was quite progressive for her age, particularly being a teenage girl in the late 40s. She stayed at the Y for one year while she studied Social Science at University to become a Social Worker. She also completed Industrial Science and Industrial Arts. Betty certainly was ahead of her time. Her parents had lived on a dairy farm in Maffra in East Gippsland, Victoria. She travelled on the train a lot, which was the way most people managed to get from place to place in those days.

She remembered paying board of 22 shillings and 6 pence per week to the Y, which was a large sum of money that had to be taken from the 25 shillings allowance she received from a university scholarship. Betty remembered Doery House being a 'pretty shabby place' with only 'reasonable' living conditions. She slept on the verandah for her year of residence as she could not afford a room in the main building. Like Marjorie's roommate she had the use of a cupboard inside another girl's room, which did not have a lock, but 'was primitive and open to theft'. Betty told me about a girl from Leongatha that often tried to get into bed with her on the verandah. Betty had led a 'sheltered life' and did not realise that the Leongatha girl was a lesbian. Many nights she had to push her out of the bed and believed this may have been one of the reasons she did not stay at the Y for a longer period as bedtime was a stressful part of the day. Betty said there was no privacy at the YWCA. She did not like 'girls who smoked' or 'smelly girls'.

The food was 'adequate but boring'. She described the matron as a 'nice old bird' but could not recall her name.

Some things never change as Betty had a boyfriend who would help her climb the balcony post and then hoist her over the rails. She laughed as she said she didn't care what he saw from his angle as long as she got back in to Doery House without being detected. Her boyfriend had a 1927 Fiat. They would go to the St. Kilda town hall dance and also have dinner sometimes in town. Her boyfriend was twelve years older and was in the air force, becoming a trainer in his career. Sadly, he died 3 years later in the English RAAF from lead poisoning. Although it appeared that Betty had encountered a somewhat sad time romantically she saw it differently as she regarded herself as having a happy life. After her first love died she married a man in the navy, but he unfortunately drowned after they were married for 8 years. They had one son. She did subsequently remarry and was married for 30 years before her third love died. Betty also had two daughters.

Betty remembered the navy or sailors making contact when a ship was in dock in Melbourne so meetings and/or dances could be arranged. She recalled the girls meeting the sailors at the dances in those days; they were never collected from the Y. Some girls were a bit wild and promiscuous.

The residents used to sit around the hedge and lawn at the front with their boyfriends waiting until the last minute to enter the Y before the front door was locked for the night. This was frowned upon by the matron, but it continued to go on no matter how much it was discouraged.

Betty played tennis on the court at the back which must have been in good condition in the late 1940s as I remembered by the mid-1960s it was unkempt and overgrown with weeds. It appeared by the state of the nets, the high wire fencing, the umpire chairs and the base surface that it was many a long year since anyone had played tennis on the courts. One was not allowed to invite a girlfriend or boyfriend to play on the courts as they were purely for residents.

The boiler room was still in place six years later as Betty also remembered having to stoke the boiler room with coke to supply the hot water for Doery House. I am thankful for the fact that this chore and antiquated way of obtaining hot water was long gone although the replacement in the shower block could hardly be classed as 'hot' water.

Betty did not like going to church as the churchgoers 'were not her type'. There was also a church service in those days at the Y if one wished to participate. She did not go home on the weekends. Sundays was always a cold meal as it was the cook's day off. She was not frightened to walk around Richmond day or night. She liked to frequent Jack Dyer's milk bar in Church Street.

Betty recalled a woman who knocked on the front door of Doery house one-night screaming 'help, help' as she was being chased by a man wielding a kitchen knife.

Betty certainly was a girl who was not letting her gender hold her back, and obviously she had the support of her parents in her desire to get a university degree and to become a social worker. This was quite an achievement in the late 1940s. She believed that the time at the YWCA was 'a valuable time to learn about people, with no family pressures and it provided a wonderful sense of freedom'.

I thought it was amazing that the passing of time had many different facets and interpretations as I could never have described the YWCA as giving me a sense of freedom but quite the contrary.

Several guys turned up to give their impressions of how life was for the girls staying at Doery House. Billy had a great memory and was willing to share lots of information about many people. His greatest memories were of Judy who lived at Simpson near Colac situated on the south-west of Melbourne. He went on to marry Judy but unfortunately their relationship didn't last. They went on dates to the trampoline centre at Hawthorn, or they would go bowling or just visit St. Kilda. They also went to Bob's hamburger bar in Bridge Road, this was a great place to eat but often teenage boys would turn up to make 'a ruckus'. Billy was born and bred in Richmond. Judy worked shift work at the PMG payroll on the corner of Bourke and Elizabeth Streets. Billy thought Judy was glad to get out of the Y and described the 'tucker as ordinary'. Judy moved to a flat in Alma Road at East St. Kilda, with her friend Chrissie and Chrissie's sister. He remembers Chrissie's sister being a very strict church goer and trying to impose her beliefs on Judy when it came to her relationship with Billy.

One of Billy's best mates also lived in Richmond, Barry whose son Simon went on to be a famous actor. Billy had lots of mates who dated YWCA girls, Ziggy; Ray; Tony; Eric dated Marg from the Riverina; Greg, Lenny and several others. Billy's nickname for the matron at the time was 'deadly' and apparently according to several others that attended the reunion that is the name used by many, particularly the males, who came in contact with the matron.

The boys would congregate outside the building. Most of the relationships were platonic and were carried on in a friendly manner. The favourite haunts for the gathering of the group was the Black Swan Coffee Shop, the International Coffee Bar, The Globe Theatre, the Vaucluse Hotel and the Swan Hotel. I wondered why I had not infiltrated this group as they sounded like a lot of fun. She had to admit to Billy that the only type of guy she seemed to attract was of an unsavoury nature which she had no desire to explore any further.

Billy's mum would often give the girls a topside roast lunch at her home in Type Street, Burnley. The girls would wash the dishes before leaving. Billy remembered many of the girls particularly Noela from the Mornington Peninsula with her beautiful red hair, and there was the free-spirited Lorna that was always the life of the party.

Billy drove a Holden FJ, which he happily informed everyone how he had 'hotted it up' and how noisy it was around the streets of Richmond.

It didn't seem to be an issue if they missed the closing time on any particular night, usually Saturday, as all the girls and guys would head over to the Jolimont Railway yards and sleep in the carriages overnight. When the cleaners came the next morning to clean the carriages for the day's use, they would all scarper before being caught. I found this story very funny, but they all agreed it was disturbing that the girls could arrive back at Doery House the following morning and no one would have realised that they did not come home the previous night. I wondered if a girl actually did not come home for several days who would notice or even if a resident didn't come home at all and simply vanished.

There didn't seem to be much compassion at Doery House amongst the hierarchy or those left in charge to look after the lonely and vulnerable. A girl from Tasmania who was slightly overweight was 'picked on' and bullied. She cried frequently and craved companionship, and appeared to be disconsolate at times. Regularly girls who cried out for companionship got love and lust confused and hence became pregnant. There was no form of birth control discussion at Doery House which would have been helpful for those who were only fifteen and quite naïve about life.

Billy's girlfriend Judy who lived at Simpson was at the Y during 1969 – 1970 living there for just over a year. She remembered having a ball at the Y and making some great friendships. She did move into a flat for approximately a year but then went back to the YWCA but this time to South Yarra. She found the food at the Y at Richmond to be 'horrible' and 'basic' with toast and vegemite for breakfast with a cup of tea. The bread that was served at dinner time was always stale. The food was very basic, but the girls ate it because they were hungry. If one arrived home after the allocated dinner time, no matter if it was just a few minutes, then a meal would not be provided even if a resident had an extenuating excuse. There was always the second-rate supper to tide one over until breakfast time. Judy was fortunate to have a single room, even if it was near the drop off area for the dirty linen. She received a very healthy wage of $47.00 per fortnight at the Post Master Generals office as a Comptometrist. I thought this was exceptional when I found out that Judy operated a machine that automatically performed mathematical processes, such as addition, subtraction, multiplication, and division, to calculate and record billing, accounting, statistical, and other numerical data. Judy then became an accounting machinist working in payroll. She loved her job, travelling to the city each day.

She recalled some moments that had stayed in her mind over the years about a girl who ran away after she found out she was pregnant; another one about an indigenous girl who was loved by everyone mostly because she had a brilliant smile and was kind to all the residents; and another girl who wore miniskirts and wigs that was so infatuated by the singer Tom Jones that every week when his program was on the television she was almost hysterical.

Judy and her friends frequented the Vaucluse Hotel in Swan Street. Some nights it was pretty noisy, and the friendly group would have to leave early if the skinheads and the mods turned up. It was preferable to leave rather than stay as sometimes fights would be stirred up and Judy's male friends did not want to be involved. They still preferred the Vaucluse though as it was more desirable than the Cherry Tree Hotel, which sadly was not a place to be patronizing if you wanted to meet certain drinking and venue standards.

Judy was able to recall one evening when they arrived back at Doery House a minute after closing time to find that as she and her friends from the Y were running down the concrete path the front door was locked in their faces at the same time as they heard the wire gate clanging shut behind them. Judy can distinctly remember hearing matron's movements inside the hostel but despite bashing on the door and pleas to the matron she would not allow the girls to come in. Judy was fortunate to have a boyfriend who was able to take her home to his mother's house. This was another example of the heartlessness often shown at the hostel when it came to looking after their charges.

Another 'boyfriend' that attended was 'Ribs' who had a wonderful nickname which he did not wish to elaborate on. He lived in Gippsland but in the 1960s he lived in Richmond. He had recollection of lots of residents, including Joy, Patsy from Mornington, Chrissy from Cranbourne, Carol, Moira and Sue. Funnily he had still retained somewhere in his brain data the YWCA phone numbers, 421927 and 421928, and the cost from a telephone box was tuppence before 1966. Ribs dated Carol for a couple of years. They would hang out at the pub or the drive-in. The Dover Castle in Bridge Road was a favourite haunt. He recalled that there was a way to re-enter the Y on the ground floor at the back. He believed the foyer at the main entrance was cold and prison like. On more than one occasion he recollected the look of the matron with her arms folded and the hardened stare. They often went out with Peter and Patsy as Ribs didn't have a car and Peter drove an enviable Ford Customline Convertible. He recalled the Beatles and the Rolling Stones music was the popular music at the time and they would sing the Beatles song 'Judy in Disguise With Glasses' to resident Judy who wore glasses. She took this in good spirit. Carol worked at Hartnell in Flinders Lane in Melbourne and described it as a 'sweat shop'. She moved to the Princess Mary Club in Lonsdale Street in the city. The descriptions of it sounded so enticing and I thoughtfully wondered why my mother had not sent me there as it was part of the Methodist Church. The tram fare from Richmond to the city was sixpence before decimal currency commenced.

Ribs confirmed that the girls hated sleeping on the verandah at Doery House as the rain came in from the west and hence they would be lucky to stay dry if the rain was accompanied by the wind. The consensus amongst those attending in the 1960s was a dislike of living at the Y but there were very few other choices that the parents of the residents would have found acceptable in those days.

Glenis is now 77 and she resided at the Y from 1956 – 1961. She had been having 'problems at home' so she arrived at Doery House at the age of fourteen. From the minute she arrived 'she loved it' after so much turmoil at home. Due to her young age she was only permitted to go out three nights per week. The matron was Mrs Rutherford and it appeared to me that she was a well-liked supervisor.

In fact, it quickly became apparent that those matrons who were married and/or had children were much more motherly and were well liked by the residents.

Glenis had spent her childhood years at Newborough in the Latrobe Valley in Victoria near Moe.

Glenis thrived on the discipline at the Y, and she said she was careful to follow the rules and regulations as she 'didn't want to go back home', but nevertheless she thought she may have managed to 'break most of them'. Glenis did venture home at one stage for approximately six months but decided she wanted to return to the hostel. Returning was not a simple procedure as she had to have a meeting with the superiors to request permission to return. She did not get on with her mother, the family had trouble making ends meet as there were nine children in the family to feed and clothe. Permission was eventually granted to return to Doery House. Glenis was 'very grateful' that she was allowed to return as she could have ended up 'with the wrong crowd' and 'getting in to trouble'.

Glenis was thankful for the 'good meals' as she was overweight due to her poor diet. She recounted that when she left Doery House she was considerably lighter than when she entered. She was gracious in emphasising that this was one of the advantages about living at the Y, and possibly it wasn't because there was less food, but It was of better quality than she had experienced at home. She was extremely good hearted about the menu while others felt they didn't receive a sufficient quantity at mealtimes. The cook at the time was Sylvia, a big lady, in her 60's with white hair. She was a 'good cook'.

If one didn't arrive at breakfast between 7.15am and 8.15am then you would 'miss out'. Porridge, cereal and toast were served, with eggs on offering once a week. One of the housekeepers was happy to sneak food to the girls if she was able to do so without being detected. As Sylvia's rostered day off was Wednesday, they had a casual cook on that day, but she only ever made stews or casseroles. Friday night was always fish and chips; this religious tradition was carried on at Doery House where they abstained from eating red meat on Fridays. It was a practice strictly adhered to by the Roman Catholic, Eastern Orthodox, Anglican and Methodist churches in those days.

Glenis confirmed the regimen in relation to those who slept each night on the verandah, of which she was one, that their wardrobe was in another room, the dresser having a 'useless lock'. She was grateful that when she returned to the Y she was moved in to a double room – apparently every girl's dream. She recalled that there was a separate student wing so that girls who were studying could have a conducive environment.

Glenis had a boyfriend but was only allowed to have a date on two nights per week, to be collected at the front door and returned to the front door upon the completion of the outing. They would go to the movies on the corner of Swan and Church Streets, would frequent The Tiger Milk Bar in Church Street and would often appear at the Trocadero in Flinders Street for a dance. The Trocadero had previously been the Green Mill dance venue where World War servicemen would meet. It was a very popular dance hall and had room for thousands of people. It had a Dutch theme with an enormous windmill. Like all the other girls she would spend time at Dimmeys and Balls buying up whatever her left over weekly money would allow.

Glenis had a friend, Fay, who got pregnant, and 'she just disappeared after that'. Glenis missed her.

Girls could be in serious trouble if they were caught talking on the telephone in an 'unladylike' manner or using conversation of a sexual nature. Mrs Rutherford could overhear the conversation on the line in the office if she so wished. All incoming calls in the late '50 went through a switchboard to Mrs Rutherford in her office, where she would then direct the call. There were phones for incoming calls near the front verandah, one on the top wing, one on the bottom wing and one in the student wing. Only the phone on the bottom floor could initiate an outgoing call and once again these calls were vetted by the matron. This telephone was always in high demand being the only facility for outgoing calls. Girls were required to limit their calls to 10 minutes, but no-one seemed to abide by this rule which only caused escalated angst amongst those waiting in the wings to call a loved one.

Glenis worked at the PMG (Post Master General) in Little Lonsdale Street on the switchboard. She caught the tram to work at a fare, she believed, of one shilling. She paid board at the YWCA of £3.16s but she was not sure what period of time this included.

Most of the attendees had an especially sad story or two. Glenis conveyed that there was a 'boy who lived across the road who was good looking' and she had asked him to a dance. She discovered that he had committed armed robbery when he held up a bookie with two other guys. She didn't know what had happened to him.

Glenis did go on to marry a boy that she dated while at the Y, the marriage lasting 18 years with the birth of two children. She never remarried.

Marriage breakups were a very common thread; was this anything to do with the environment the girls lived in while they were teenagers or was it just the way life evolved for all sectors of the population no matter where they had lived as adolescents.

Maybe Glenis crossed paths, without knowing it, with Lorna who resided at the YWCA during 1961 – 1963 at the age of 18. Her family lived at Wesburn in Victoria, east of Melbourne, a short distance from Warburton.

She had worked in the office at Kaysers Lingerie. She walked to work as it was only a short distance. She was grateful for this as she knew a lot of girls spent much of their weekly pay packet on tram and train fares.

The menu had obviously not changed at the Y as

Lorna also experienced cereal, porridge and toast for breakfast. To this day she dislikes egg and bacon pie as it was served far too frequently in the dining room. She made some good friends, Coralie, who went to the movies with her, also to the botanical gardens and the Moomba Festival to see the parade and the many things that happened on the river, especially the water skiing. Marie, Margaret and Sue introduced her to Norman who was a tow truck driver. They used public transport to get around; he would often take her on picnics and to visit his mother in Prahran. They would go to the dances at Glenferrie.

Not all residents were of an amiable nature though, as one girl used to steal Lorna's mail from the incoming post board where the mail was held in by large pieces of criss-cross elastic. The girl would taunt her with the mail and on one occasion she burnt a letter from Lorna's mother.

Lorna recalled a staff member who was liked very much by the girls dying of cancer.

Lorna read a lot in her spare time. She played tennis but not at the Y. She only went home once a month as that was all she was allowed. Lorna was fortunate enough to reside and sleep in a double room. She remembered vividly the 'peeping toms' that came around and someone exposing themselves; 'a flasher'. Men would come in the front gate and down the path then peer in the windows. She did not like walking around Richmond. She once went on a blind date, but when her date and his mate started 'playing up' she decided to leave them but after losing sight of the guys she was followed by a car. She was absolutely petrified; her heart was racing and so she started to run and was so appreciative when some pedestrians appeared who scared off the stalker. This was another story that was common amongst the girls, where they all seemed to have a recollection of something that happened to them that was traumatic.

The residents of the hostel would have felt the experiences particularly harshly and with great impact as most had come from small country towns where the realities of city life were not exposed to them. They had been cosseted by their families and friends, where the towns people had looked after their own and generally cared for each other. Life in the city and the surrounding suburbs were frightening, not only for me, but for many of the girls whether they were residents at Doery House during the '40s, '50s or '60s. These observations, involvements and struggles would also have made an enormous impression on the future shaping of all the girls.

Of all those who attended the reunion, June had the most phenomenal recollections of her time at the YWCA in Richmond. She had come from Cowes on Phillip Island. When she first left home she went to the Presbyterian Girls Hostel at Elsternwick but it closed in the Spring of 1957 and the 20 – 30 girls who resided there were informed that if they had nowhere else to go then the YWCA at Richmond would take them. June resided at Doery House from 1957 – 1959, but at the end of that period she was required to move to the YWCA facility at South Yarra as the hostel was converted in to a junior residence only, and as June was 19 she would be required to move out. She paid weekly board of £3 10s.

Along with Richmond and South Yarra there were other YWCA facilities for girls at Elwood and Footscray.

In the time June was there she was overseen by two matrons, Mrs Rutherford who was very strict and Mrs Thompson who was more forgiving. Mrs Thompson did magnificent needlework in her office in the evening. She was more motherly than Mrs Rutherford. Miss Isobel Kolevas and Miss Delaney from the YWCA in Melbourne would visit regularly to conduct a house meeting in the lounge room where residents could air any concerns they were encountering. This definitely did not occur when I was in residence, as there were many grievances then that the girls could have shared with management. The head office for the YWCA was in Russell Street Melbourne. It was a red brick structure with a wide arch over the entrance steps into the building. Miss Delaney was the hostel superintendent who appeared to have seniority over the matrons. She was middle aged, with short grey hair and wore plain tailored grey suits with a white blouse; her feet were encased in sensible black flat shoes. She had a kindly 'plain' face and was a 'no frills gal'.

June first worked as a secretary completing shorthand, typing and other duties including duplicating on a Gestetner machine at F. W. Cheshire in Little Collins Street. They were a large basement bookstore. It was a very successful publishing house and produced educational textbooks in the 1950s. After a couple of years, she moved on to employment in a small office and as a sign of the times she stayed there until she retired in 1963 when she was expecting her first child. The first pay packet was cash in a small beige envelope containing £5 and threepence. Cash in a small beige envelope seemed to be the way all the girls were paid. For June every birthday she would receive a pay rise. Mr Cheshire was a devout Christian and would give all the staff a bonus at Christmas and Easter. By the time June was eighteen she was earning £8 which was a considerable amount of money. When she moved to her new employer she was earning £10 without any Saturday work, hence I imagined she was a very experienced and competent worker.

Her best friends were Janice and Carol. They loved classical music and spent much time listening to 3LO which would broadcast the ABC symphony orchestra concerts at the Melbourne Town Hall. Janice came from Port Campbell and worked at Allans Music store in Collins Street near the Hotel Australia. She obviously enjoyed and appreciated classical music as she played the cello. The girls remember being asked to do some gardening at the hostel and were actually paid for this chore to be completed. It seemed amazing that the matron didn't expect it to be completed ex gratia.

She recalled that at one time they allegedly had a

snowdropper as many of the girls were losing their underwear from the clothesline.

In the main living area there was a piano, table tennis table, a radiogram and records. My friends and I could not recollect this so maybe they had been removed before we resided there.

June confirmed many of the happenings that others had conveyed at the get together. There were about one hundred residents when she was there.

She was only locked out once but being savvy she sat at the end of the verandah for over an hour praying another girl would be coming in with a late key. Fortunately, this occurred, and she was rescued from an isolated night outdoors. I thought this was a great idea but probably wouldn't have liked to take my chances as it would be a long, cold night if no one came along.

The double storey boarding house across the road housed all males and the girls knew that some had binoculars, but with the heavy canvas blind rolled down on the verandah from the top to the handrail June believed they would not have been successful with their viewing expeditions.

The matron's room was at the top of the stairs on the left.

When she moved to a single room, which I thought must have been luxurious, she had a view of the spire at St. John's Toorak.

June did a lot of sewing on the hostel sewing machines buying her requirements at Balls. She even made an evening dress from blue satin and white lace. She used Simplicity sewing patterns. She bought a pair of white satin court shoes with fashionable pointy toes and a small heel in 1960 at Dimmeys for her wedding costing nine shillings and eleven pence.

On Saturday nights some of the girls would run along the corridors at Doery House calling out 'anyone for the Masonic?' Then June and a group of other girls would go in to the Masonic Lodge in Collins Street for the weekly dance in the ballroom. Dances were called 50-50 which was a mix of Foxtrot, Pride of Erin, Barn Dance, Evening Three Step and Modern Waltz. The girls loved the barn dance as changing partners throughout the dance gave them a chance to meet a prospective new boyfriend. They were not afraid to catch the tram to and from the dance as there was a large group of them.

It became apparent that Dr Roseby had helped many girls in their time at the YWCA. I could never recall him making 'house' visits to the hostel but June recalled a resident named Lorraine who was hallucinating one night and had severe blisters on parts of her body, particularly the backs of her legs, hence Dr Roseby was called, who found she had severe sunstroke and dehydration after falling asleep on the beach during a Melbourne heatwave. June recalled the red light at the entrance to Dr Roseby's gateway which was common for doctors to display in those days.

Trust was a big part of life in the 1950s. A Sri Lankan girl, Kusuma, was returning to live with her family after residing at the YWCA. The 'SS Himalaya' was leaving from Port Melbourne and visitors were welcome to board the ship to farewell family and friends before they departed. One wonders if there were ever any stowaways.

June did meet the love of her life while she was at Richmond. They met at a youth camp in 1958.

EPILOGUE

WHAT HAPPENED TO ME, SHIRLEY AND OLIVIA?

I continued successfully with my dental nursing career in Melbourne. I lived in various places with various people which did include Shirley and Olivia.

I went to a party with Shirley one day in 1971 and met my future husband. We married in 1973 and I was very happy. Shirley was in the bridal party. My husband's employer wanted him to move to South Australia. My beautiful new car had to be sold as my husband needed a new car for himself. This left me in a new state without a job and without a car. He travelled all over the state.

I had assorted dental nursing jobs, but transport was a problem and I often found myself after a long day on my feet walking extremely long distances in the dark after missing the last bus home.

To fill in time I studied to become a dental radiographer and finally landed a job with a wonderful employer. My elderly next-door neighbour saw how lonely I was and gave me a little old Morris Minor car.

Next came the birth of my first child.

Five years had passed from the time of arrival in South Australia and it was time to pack up and leave everything behind to move to Queensland. This place was worse than the last and more loneliness came with it.

Another child arrived.

I found it difficult to make friends in the early days and depression was my friend. I was often on my own due to my husband's never-ending travel. I wanted to work, and I wanted another child. My family lived in another state. I missed my mother terribly.

I married for a second time in 1989.

My family were furious, particularly my mother, who for years pounded me verbally with negative comments. When my mother passed away her massive pile of diaries was given to me by my youngest sister. In these I discovered that my mother, over many, many years, had written about her strong displeasure at my path in life. The diaries also uncovered the lengths family members had gone to in the quest to tear down any friendships I had, in an apparent attempt to make my life as unhappy as possible. My father told all the other members of the family to 'move on' as I was obviously happy.

I had a job now in my partner's business. So many people said it would not last but after 32 years we are still together and happily married.

I have 2 wonderful, high achieving children and 5 delightful grandchildren.

I managed a blended family with my partner with varying degrees of success.

I worked right up until my mid-sixties, studying during

that time to upskill my knowledge in both business administration and management. I had a variety of jobs after my second husband sold his business in 2004.

I have 4 siblings but only have contact with 1 of them. I have a fractured relationship with 2 of my sisters and my darling brother was chased so long by the 'black dog' that he finally gave up and took his own life in 2008. My mother died from a lung condition after an extremely protracted illness in 2003 aged 72. Ten days before her death she held my hand and said 'you know I always loved you' as a tear rolled down her cheek.

My father died of leukaemia in 2012 after a short illness aged 82.

I stayed in Queensland and am very happy living by the water.

My love of sewing never waned which included intricate embroidery often spun together with quilts, frequently of an artistic nature.

I was diagnosed with Lymphoma in 2017 but am currently in remission.

The little wooden church, in Upper Beaconsfield, that my great grandfather built was burnt to the ground in the Ash Wednesday bushfires on 16 February 1983.

****

Shirley left Doery House in mid-1970 to share a flat with her older sister who was a newly graduated nurse.

She had a public service job and was reasonably well paid. Her family life was a big worry as her mother and father were still living in SA with her younger brother. Shirley's father (a WW2 veteran) was an addicted gambler and her mother was in denial, blaming their troubles on other things. Her mother was not coping and there was no way to help even though Shirley tried, and continued to do so for the rest of her mother's life She believed she looked after her parents – they did not look after their family. They eventually divorced and her mother returned to Melbourne, but she had mental health problems, which of course were not recognised in the 1970s. Her father died from prostate cancer and her mother died of cancer only 3 years later – they were both only 67 years old.

Like me, Shirley was lonely, even living with her sister, as her sister worked shift work and was also studying. She felt guilty that she was not continuing her education as the Public Service offered part-time study, but she felt she needed support from her family.

In the early 1970s Shirley decided to go to ballroom dancing classes as that provided social activities that were easy to access using public transport. She met a group of young people and ended up marrying a member of that group. I was a bridesmaid at her wedding. She thought that her life would be much more productive as a wife - but she was wrong.

Married life was also lonely – her husband was married to his family business and although they lived in a very nice house in an upmarket neighbourhood she knew there was something missing.

Shirley had three children and life rolled on until her 40th birthday, when her husband gave her a very expensive "surprise" party which she felt was more about him than her, judging by the venue and the invitees.

She realised that she had relationship issues which took them to counselling. This turned out to be a horrible process because she was trying so hard to work through their differences and her husband was not being honest during the counselling. Eventually he divulged that he had been sexually abused as a young man and after this revelation Shirley felt that she had to support him. She tried to make things work but could not keep up the pretence to the outside world that they were a happy couple. She realised that her husband was gay and asked him to leave.

Shirley was exhausted emotionally. Her children were baffled as their father was not forthcoming with any explanation. He has been in a same sex relationship for many years now.

Shirley had not worked since having children, so it was necessary to find courses of low cost or no cost, aiming to help women back into the workforce. She found a new job in the year that she turned 60 which boosted her confidence.

The family home was eventually sold, and she managed to obtain a settlement that covered the purchase of a suitable property in a neighbouring suburb, since then she has moved again into a smaller property.

Shirley had one other long-term relationship but was reluctant to give up her hard-won independence. Shirley believes her three children are very competent, well-educated, independent children. Although she has no nieces and nephews she gets pleasure from her two grandchildren.

Shirley's sister loved her nursing and went on to become a qualified nurse, midwife, infant welfare sister and teacher. She worked overseas and in regional Australia. She did not marry nor have children. She retired to regional Victoria but unfortunately did not have long to enjoy her hard-earned retirement. She died at age 66 yrs.

Shirley's brother got through the tough times and is now a Community Support worker in a regional area. He has not had children.

Shirley believes that marriage break-ups, and relationships that do not last, mean the loss of friends and acquaintances, as does changing jobs. It's important to have some anchors in friends with whom you feel comfortable because they just "know you". Those friends are Olivia and me.

Shirley finds it is still very upsetting to think that much of what happened at the YWCA was allowed to happen without any other adult person stepping in to provide assistance.

****

Olivia left the YWCA and returned to the country town where she was born to work in the local bank for four years. She continued her relationship with the boy she had met during her school years and they moved to Melbourne in 1972. This was the same boy who took up so much time on the telephone at the YWCA.

Once again she lived with Shirley and me for a short time prior to her marriage. We were her bridesmaids at the wedding in September 1972. Olivia and her husband lived in Elwood and Seaford for 4 years.

They had a son in 1976 and following a devastating fire in her husband's parents sawmill they returned to the country area to rebuild and manage the sawmill.

They built a lovely house there and lived close to her in-laws.

In 1980 they had a second son and that year Olivia's father passed away.

In 1981 they had a third son.

Olivia worked in the business day and night and also to assist with income she started a lawn mowing and gardening business and also a catering business. The funds were required as her husband was spending far too much time at the local hotel, the football club and a service club. She was virtually bringing up the children on her own by now and dealing with a very aggressive alcoholic.

Her only escape was the many community groups she was involved in.

By 1985 the marriage was near the end.

Olivia developed a relationship with the chap who did the truck deliveries into the building and hardware business.

In such a small town she was labelled a scarlet woman, as all the old town locals loved her ex-husband and his family, but little did they know what happened behind closed doors.

People would cross to the other side of the street if they saw Olivia approaching.

She remarried in 1987 wearing a red dress. They built a house on land given to them by his parents.

Their daughter was born in 1988.

By 1989 Olivia was helping with the delivery of goods to businesses within a 100km radius, with her daughter in a car seat beside her in the truck. Life was hectic once more as she was also working at night in the business.

Her mother passed away in 1989 followed by her eldest brother who was only 54 years old.

When her daughter was about 4 her father bought her a Shetland pony and that started an interest in horses that was never going to disappear. She started Pony Club, just up the road, when she was 8. This was the beginning of future problems.

Due to a number of factors Olivia and her second husband decided to walk away from the business and sell the trucks and anything related to transport. They both found other work.

Olivia's daughter was now competing in Pony Club events, was a state junior in the EFA squad and competing with the HRCAV, all over Victoria.

Olivia started full-time work in the office at the local supermarket.

The family now had a horse truck and two mad keen people in the house that breathed, ate and slept horses. They had 4 horses in the paddocks at that stage and competitions took up most weekends each year. It was admirable having all the horses and the events that went with them, but horses and competitions require extreme amounts of funds.

In 2003 the debts were mounting up and the only option would be to sell the house and the horses. Olivia's husband refused to consider this.

Olivia does not know the reason why she thought what proceeded would be a good idea, but she decided to help herself to some of the takings from her employer at the supermarket business where she was employed. She proceeded to alter book-keeping figures to cover up her actions.

This continued for 3 years in an effort to cover the horse expenses. She lived in a time warp during that time, watching the bills roll in and working out how much she would need to steal the following week as they now had a bigger horse truck and even more horses.

In early 2005 Olivia had an accident in the horse truck and rolled it over, killing 1 horse and maiming 2 others. Her daughter was with her and she never forgave her mother for this mishap.

The Victorian horse community held a fund raiser for the family, donating over $4,000 towards the vet bills and extra costs, but the vet bills totalled over $10,000, and this was despite the fact that they then had to get another larger horse truck and more horses.

So, she continued to steal from her employers, it was now up to about $1,000 per week. Something had to give.

On Olivia's birthday in June 2006 she went to her employers and told them what she had been doing for the past 3 years. Naturally the police were called to the business and she was charged with theft and fraud by deception. The total she had stolen was just under $130,000.

A bigger shock was to come Olivia's way, as within 48 hours her husband and daughter chose to wipe their hands of her. All that she had done wrong was all for nothing. Love can be so shallow. She felt she had done all she could to maintain their love of horses and when she needed them most they deserted her.

She sold everything she had, borrowed from her family, cashed in her superannuation and managed to repay her former employers within 9 months.

She was fortunate to obtain employment within 6 weeks. She divulged the whole story at her job interview.

Olivia's 3 sons were amazing and could not have been more supportive, but most of her friends abandoned her. It was difficult to tell family and friends what she had done, when she was struggling to understand why she had done it herself.

Olivia rang me to inform me of her double life.

'You are not going to want to be my friend anymore,' she said

'Why, have you killed someone?' I replied

'No,'

'Then I will always be your friend. Now tell me what has happened' I responded

Eventually Olivia could move away from the bigots in her hometown. Her eldest son, who was living in Sydney, suggested that he move back to Melbourne so they could share accommodation, which they did. The moving day was the last time she ever had any conversation or contact with her daughter.

Olivia's court case was in March 2007 and she was given a suspended sentence and to be of good behaviour for 3 years. This lighter suspended sentence appeared to be due to many reasons including some excellent character references, the fact that she had paid all the money back that she had stolen, and that she had gone to her employers to confess.

Olivia's barrister made sure the case was heard in a country county court so that it would not be put in the national newspapers. She later paid another $30,000 to her former employers for their legal costs and she paid a further $10,000 in legal fees for herself. Olivia said she was now completely broke but didn't care as she still had most of her family, her true friends, a roof over her head, good health and most importantly her sanity back.

She is now a criminal and will be listed as one until the day she dies.

She has had several jobs and has always been honest with her past.

One job held extra happiness where she met the man who is her partner now.

She has met new people and started living the life she had always enjoyed before 2003.

In 2012 she moved suburbs to be with her partner and she chanced upon a job opportunity to work as a travel consultant (not bad at 61 years of age), a career she had always dreamed of.

Olivia lost her last remaining sibling in 2013 aged 69 years.

She feels she is blessed with wonderful sons, grandchildren, a job she is passionate about with so many opportunities to travel (except to the USA, who do not allow criminals to visit there), also good friends who she values and a treasured partner.

She has no contact with her daughter and the child she has since had, but she accepts this as part of the consequences of the decisions she made in her life.

****

Miss Dorothy Lamrock died in 1975 at the age of 67, approximately 5 years after Shirley, Olivia and I left Doery House. She had 3 siblings, none of whom married nor had children, so she neither had children of her own nor any nieces or nephews.

Maybe her outlook on life was coloured by some of the tragedy in her life. Her mother died when Dorothy was 33 years old, her brother tragically died when she was 25 and her Auntie unfortunately died when Dorothy was 25 years old.

Many unanswered questions remain.

What brought an elderly lady without children to be in charge of some 100 teenagers in the late 1960s and to treat them in such a harsh manner?

Were the hierarchy at the YWCA aware of the

conditions or the treatment metered out?

Why was the environment so harsh when the price to live in the residence was so costly?

****

Doery House was listed for sale in 1991. The information in the sales article said "the accommodation is basic, with rooms measuring about three metres by three metres and were like cells, the rooms had seen better days. All 88 rooms need refurbishment."

It was refurbished and eventually became Richmond Hill Hotel.

****

By the late '60s it seemed the world was spinning a little faster as teenage girls followed new trends, changed as the fashion did, sought at every opportunity a more colourful and energetic version of almost everything for themselves and their way of living. The spirit and thirst for transformation seemed limitless.

They wanted to be the very best they could be in all phases of their lives. And so, they forged on past their teenage years to become adults.

****

Some friendships do last forever. Shirley Olivia and I meet annually despite not all residing in the same state. Our friendship held fast even in the most trying times. We would spend many days together always using our signature motto "Girls Just Want to Have Fun".

ACKNOWLEDGEMENTS

Thank you to my dear and trusted friends Jan Rattray and Jan Brooks. This book would not have been possible without your insight, knowledge and encouragement.

This book would not exist without these two wonderful friends. It was you who made me think seriously about putting my story in to words and then on to paper. This book wasn't easy to write. It was difficult bringing back the past that I had hoped would never resurface. Thanks for helping me get the details right and for encouraging me to find my voice. I respect you both for opening up about your feelings and your lives.

To Dr Lisette Dillon, my Beta Reader I give you high praise. Not only did you evaluate the book and provide valuable feedback, but you gently nudged me towards publication. You always believed in me and the book. You have become a loyal friend. It has been a joy to work with you.

Thank you for the true gift of friendship to Jan Rattray. You completed the first proof reading of the book. I pay tribute to your time and energy with this project. You listened, enthused and were a faithful constant. Your support and help throughout the years will never be forgotten.

A special thanks to Beverley McDonald who is a master of punctuation and sentence structure. You completed the work with passion and enthusiasm. I am extremely fortunate to have had your input.

My children never wavered with their enthusiasm and moral support.

Thank you to all the enthusiastic and caring people at The Redcliffe Writers and the Fellowship of Australian Writers Queensland (FAWQ). A special mention to Jim Higgins who encouraged me to publish the book following a special reading of the first chapter at a function in 2019.

I am indebted to the Richmond Historical Society and in particular David Langdon. Whenever I required information or clarification you were accommodating and willing to oblige in any manner. You helped me gather vital information.

I thank all those people for responding to my requests for information after the Melbourne Herald Sun published an article in their 'Desperately Seeking' column. You bravely and selflessly agreed to share your stories and relive experiences from the past. I believe some of you thought the book would never be published.

I would like to thank the past residents of the YWCA at Richmond. I would like to pay tribute to your efforts to be heard, and to recognise your battles.

A special thanks to Russell Perry from Perry Digital Marketing who helped me navigate the complexities of preparing a book for publishing. You listened to me and managed to place my thoughts succinctly on the cover. You provided assistance through the minefield of requirements. I thank you for being so calm and understanding.

A big thank you goes to all the people who have reached this page and have read my story.

Lastly, but by no means the least, my sincere thanks goes to my patient, abundantly kind and caring husband, Rod. You never gave up on your encouragement as I brought this story to life and battled the demons of the past. You believed that my story needed to be told so that readers may gain a sense of understanding of the establishment and that period of time.

BIBLIOGRAPHY

Janet McCalman, 'Struggle Town – Public and Private Life in Richmond 1990-1995' (New ed.) (South Melbourne, Hyland House, 1998)

Catherine Watson, 'Copping it Sweet: Shared Memories of Richmond' (Melbourne, City of Richmond, Carringbush Regional Library, 1988)

Morag Loh (ed.), 'Growing up in Richmond' (Richmond, Vic. Richmond Community Education Centre, 1979)

Various web sites.

Made in the USA
Columbia, SC
11 October 2020